D1520811

One of the most important tasks for a CEO is to shape the senior team into a cohesive, high functioning unit. This gets done through the hard work of learning how each person on the team consumes information, makes decisions, and communicates their ideas. Jeanne Johnson showed me in her book that the work of team building is not done when you leave the office, and all of us can contribute to a greater good by building up great teams in our families and communities. The most important first step is to park your agenda and listen.

- Alex Shootman, CEO & author of *Done Right: How Tomorrow's Top Leaders Get Stuff Done*

If You Love Me You'll Listen To Me is a direct from the heart narrative bursting with countless useful tips that teaches readers how to be effective communicators and wholehearted listeners. Jeanne Johnson has written a wonderful book that combines a lifetime of experiences, along with research and advice from experts, into an informative, engaging guide that empowers her readers to care for themselves, while also learning how to be better partners/parents/ friends/coworkers/neighbors.

- Frank Mortimer, author of *Bee People And The Bugs They Love*

Jeanne Johnson cuts through the distracting and deafening noise of our busy culture to reteach us one of the most important and simple truths about communication -- active listening is the key to better relationships and productive connection. If you want to be more present, intentional and empowered, create the space and time to enjoy If You Love Me You'll Listen to Me.

- Karen Latimer, MD Family Physician & Parenting Coach & author of *Take Back the House - Raising Happy Parents*

IF YOU LOVE ME, YOU'LL LISTEN TO ME

How to Find Peace Through Compassionate Listening

Jeanne Hope Johnson

Publishing

This book is dedicated to the three most important people in my life. Each has changed me for the better.

My good fortune to have met and married Jeff still amazes me. If I could design the ideal partner, I couldn't have created anyone more perfect.

My daughter Laura—my idol. Her love of and passion for this planet and her desire to seek justice for the marginalized impress, inform, and inspire me daily.

My son Drew—the optimist. His first word was happy. His kindness, compassion, and dedication to contributing good to society will always motivate me.

It's a genuine privilege to walk through life alongside these extraordinary individuals.

I am forever grateful. xoxo

Table of Contents

Foreword

D o you ever feel like you're not being heard or that your ideas and opinions aren't taken seriously? Do you wonder if your words and feelings matter to others?

This book is for you if you want more confidence and personal fulfillment and long to experience more joy. It will help you discover how to become more self-assured, happier, healthier, and filled with goodwill toward others. No matter who you are or your current situation, regardless of your age, culture, beliefs, or religion, the insights within these pages will help you find your voice and teach you how to listen to yourself and the world around you. This book will act as a guide, advising you and teaching you how to fulfill your life's purpose.

Jeanne Johnson is a loving, influential, and powerful leader. She has lived all over the United States, spearheading and managing multi-dimensional goodwill projects along the way, which have earned her countless awards, certificates, and accolades. She speaks from her heart about creating meaningful connections and is a true example of what you can become when you apply yourself and give to the greater good.

Jeanne shares personal experiences to help you build confidence, overcome anxieties, and be available to others. She believes that what you get from life and how you conduct yourself is your decision and your responsibility. This book will help you adjust to the environment you deserve and assist you in managing your thoughts, emotions, and actions. Get ready to read this inspiring journey, prepare for massive change in your relationships, and tap into peace.

Raymond Aaron
New York Times **Bestselling Author**

Introduction

Have you ever been speaking, and no matter what you do, you keep getting interrupted? You start saying a sentence, and suddenly, someone jumps in to finish it. Even if the person is on target with your thoughts, it's frustrating when they interrupt. What's worse is when your half-finished idea is taken in an entirely different direction than what was intended. It's so irritating!! Interrupting conversations causes strained relationships, disconnection, anger, and resentment, and no one wants that. Everyone wants to feel heard, and all of us are on a journey of self-expression. One of my journeys has been to impact the world positively. But, if I'm honest, my intentions haven't always turned out well. Too often, I've taken it upon myself to "fix" things that are, frankly, none of my business. I have been known to infuse my opinion into all sorts of matters. It took a severe toll on my relationships, particularly with my family.

I call my husband and myself the King and Queen of Interruptus. We are also the parents of the Prince and Princess of Interruptus. The four of us have jokingly batted these titles around for years, but none truly understood how our interruptions impacted our family. The revelation of this reality was a real trigger point of change in my life.

The summer before our daughter graduated from high school, we went on a road trip to research colleges. It was a bittersweet adventure. We spent hours in the car reminiscing about our years together and collectively dreaming of what would come. At one point, we got on the subject of how my husband and I are control freaks. I wasn't shocked that the kids saw us in that light, but when my husband agreed that I was unbearable at times, it surprised me. Feeling stunned, I pointed out the many times he'd been insufferably opinionated, and on and on it went. Finally, to resolve the conflict, I Googled, "What is a control freak?"

A person who feels an obsessive need to exercise control over themselves and others and to take command of any situation.

At first, I didn't recognize myself in this definition but, unsurprisingly, my children and I saw many of these traits in my husband. We jokingly decided we wanted to help him become a better person by pointing out his flaws. It didn't occur to us that this fun exercise might hurt his feelings. He retaliated by saying, "You guys always interrupt me." Soon his favorite phrase became, "I'm sorry for talking while you are interrupting." His comment made me admit that I interrupt quite a bit, which helped me realize how rude it is and how important it is to change. I recognized that listening has a powerful effect on people. When we listen attentively, people can hear the truth in themselves, often for the first time. Generous listening expands conversations. It is one of the most valuable gifts we can give one another. When we don't offer such a simple gesture, it can profoundly affect the people we care about.

My friend described it this way: "I was in pain and tried to pour my heart out, but the person I was talking to kept interrupting me and telling me that they had a similar story and offering me advice. I felt frustrated because they wouldn't listen to me. When people do this, I feel stupid, like what I say isn't important. It makes me feel like a nuisance, annoying, and not worth their time."

Someone else said, "When people interrupt me, it makes me feel like they don't care about me. It's very frustrating to be in a conversation with someone who interrupts. It's like they think their opinion is most important." These comments helped me decide to take off my Queen of Interruptus crown and work at becoming the Queen of Effective Listening. It's a work in progress, but it has changed my life.

The reality is that some people interrupt because it's how they process and interpret information. In their enthusiasm to show they're on the same wavelength, they interrupt and ironically sabotage their effort to connect with you. They don't mean to be rude or disrespectful; quite the opposite, they are actively engaged in what you're saying and want to prove that they understand, so they complete the sentence for you. If you're a conversationalist who gives long pauses between thoughts, you might unknowingly be inviting this interrupting behavior. Sometimes, people interrupt because they think a break in talking is an invitation to satisfy the void. Or they believe they need to help find the words you're trying to find. They fill in the blanks and the dead air with thoughts they think you're trying to express. Other times, people are rushed and need to speed up communication and get on to other tasks. Interrupting is their way of keeping the conversation moving. They are so pressed for time that they are oblivious to how they are potentially damaging their relationships. Sometimes, people interrupt because they are frustrated. If they've tried several times to speak up and are ignored, they may resort to interrupting. It's a natural response, and we all do it from time to time, but we should all strive to give the people we care about our undivided attention during conversations.

Communication is the cornerstone of healthy and long-lasting relationships, and with that comes good listening skills. Active listening helps people feel understood, which is a fundamental need. When we feel understood, amazing feelings develop, and human connections deepen. So please, become passionate about compassionate communication. Every day, exhibit empathy and authenticity to yourself and others, and together, we can build a kinder and more connected society. I am grateful that you picked up this book and will be even more thankful if you take the time to read it and put it to use.

CHAPTER ONE

Generous Listening Works

*"There is a difference between listening
and waiting for your turn to speak."*
~ Simon Sinek

These days, compassion is being promoted as the answer to everything—from greater productivity in the workplace to harmony on the home front to healing fractured communities and finding inner peace. These claims are backed up by a steady stream of research from universities such as Stanford, Berkeley, Harvard, and others. Neuroscientists and psychologists are confirming something that has been at the center of the world's great religious traditions for the ages. That is the core value of cultivating a strong, loving heart. And who can't stand behind that? As I began to listen to others with more compassion, I noticed two things change. My marriage improved, and my relationship with my kids became more engaging. The bond I have with my husband has deepened and grown more sacred. We've created a safe place to share our dreams, desires, fears, and frustrations. As we generously listen to one another, we're building a bond of trust that grows stronger daily. But none of this came naturally to either of us. We had to get help because our interrupting and resentments were tearing us apart. We both sensed that we might not stay together if we didn't do something about our communication styles.

I researched and found an incredible couple's retreat. It took place on a glorious summer weekend in the Berkshire Mountains in Massachusetts. I figured if the lessons didn't stick, we could at least have a good time hiking. Thankfully, neither of us wanted to spend time in the woods because both of us became completely mesmerized by what we were learning. The workshop was called "Getting the Love You Want: A Guide for Couples." It was facilitated by *New York Times* bestselling author Dr. Harville Hendricks and his wife, Dr. Helen LaKelly Hunt. In their opening comments, they promised that we were about to have a life-changing experience. My husband and I rolled our eyes and laughed because we didn't think a three-day retreat could accomplish such lofty claims. But many years later, we still recognize that weekend as one of the most profound encounters of our married life.

In the workshop, we discovered that talking is the most dangerous thing people do. Listening is the scariest and the rarest thing we do because if we listen, we might hear something that dismisses our point of view on how the world works. My husband and I realized that we weren't alone and that most people can't talk about their differences or needs without going into polarization with others. We also found out that conflict isn't destructive in a relationship; the problem with conflict is that people wait too long to solve it. Studies have shown that it takes an average of four hours to call 911 when people have physical heart pains. When we experience emotional heartbreak or unrest, it takes an average of seven years to address it. By then, the problem is so big it's almost impossible to get to the root of it. Harville and Helen helped my husband and me realize that conflict resolution is actually pretty simple. In fact, it's so simple this stuff can – and should – be taught in elementary school.

Dr. Hendricks and Dr. LaKelly Hunt are the founders of Imago Relationship Therapy, a form of couples counseling and coaching designed to help relationship partners work out misunderstandings, reduce conflict, and rediscover ways to bond, communicate, and generally find common ground. A primary goal of the Imago approach is to help partners stop blaming, criticizing, and negatively reacting to each other. The technique aims to help couples listen deeply to each other's concerns and needs, develop empathy and understanding, and help heal from past experiences and past relationships – the ones we had with our parents and other prominent guiding forces in our personal development as a child.

Very specific techniques are used in Imago Relationship Therapy: dialogue, mirroring, validation, and empathy. Imago dialogue is a structured process that allows two people to understand one another better, resulting in empathy. The goals are to remove hurtful negative language from communication patterns, create a safe place that allows couples the space to create an equal partnership, and do away with an imbalance of power, providing a safe environment to share freely.

Mirroring involves repeating back to your partner what you just heard them say. This technique clarifies and also ensures that you understand what was said. Mirroring is done without judgment or criticism; instead, you simply repeat what you heard your partner say.

Validation is key when it comes to Imago Relationship Therapy. By validating what your partner has shared or said, you let them know that you understand where they're coming from. If you don't truly understand them or what they're saying, then offering validation can let them know that you're at least trying.

Empathy is the final part of the process. This is where you share what you think your partner might be feeling and lets them know you have a very clear, in-depth understanding of the emotional experience they might be going through.

The method has taught my husband and me how to have safe conversations. We practice (almost) daily and have found that it breaks the cycle of destructive discussions we have been engaging in. When we talk now, we allow the other to listen with compassion. We've learned not to deliver monologues or parallel monologues – I talk, you talk, I talk, you talk – and we focus instead on a lateral way of speaking to one another. Doing this helps us process what the other person says. As a result, we create connecting conversations that are random and fulfilling. This way of communicating is indigenous to human nature and a helpful tool when sharing our thoughts with others. What's not common nowadays is slowing down and taking steps to listen to understand other people. The simple process of taking turns talking and listening in a structured way works with every relationship. Dr. LaKelly Hunt and Dr. Hendricks recognized that their successful Imago Relationship Therapy technique should be taught to as many people as possible. Eventually, they began teaching Safe Conversation workshops and sharing the life-changing process with the broader community. We will go into that a little deeper later in the book.

Using the Safe Conversation method dramatically changed how I engage with our children. I shifted away from judgment to curiosity and wonder. It has made a profound difference in how we relate to one another. My relationship with my kids is much more open and engaging now. They feel safe sharing themselves with me. As a result, I've learned a great deal about how they see the world. The respect and admiration I have for them are indescribable. If I hadn't learned to offer them my focused attention, I don't think they would trust me, and I don't think they would feel comfortable sharing their feelings with me. These are the rewards for listening and being curious.

Parents and kids are often on different wavelengths, whether the kids are children or grown adults. Using the principles of talking without criticism, listening without judgment, and genuinely connecting beyond our differences helps prevent and improve mental and physical health issues. It aids productivity, school performance and achievement, and individual and family economics. It can also help avoid anxiety, depression, addictions such as alcohol and drug use, breakdowns in the family, and absenteeism from school and the workplace. When we listen to our kids, we are communicating to them that they are worthy of our attention. If we validate their distress, we demonstrate that their point of view has merit, and by allowing them time to decide their course of action, we indicate that we trust their problem-solving abilities. Active listening truly is the single most important skill we can have in our parenting "toolbelt." But be patient with yourself. It is a very sophisticated skill that can take years to master. I am nowhere near that because I, like most people, wasn't raised in a home where this kind of listening was practiced. And very little of it occurs in our fast-paced, solution-oriented society, so learning how to do it is much like learning a second language. It is no wonder that it can feel forced, unnatural, and uncomfortable when beginning to practice this skill. But listening to what our children say is the only way we can build a strong bond with them. If we want them to know they are important to us, we must give them our focused attention. Staying quiet while they are speaking and making eye contact with them is critical. It is rare for kids to bare their souls to their parents, especially during the tween and teenage stages. When we engage in thoughtful listening and non-judgmental dialog, they learn to trust us. When we are "all in" during conversations, the information we get and the unfolding of emotions are astonishing. Being completely present means listening to the words being shared, watching their body language, and feeling their emotions. Being an active listener doesn't mean you can't talk yourself, but being patient and present shows your child that you really care what they have to say. Listening to your child doesn't mean that you will always agree with them, but it will give them a sense of respect. When we are entirely available during discussions, we create a safe place for them to be their authentic selves. It goes without saying that generous listening is the most validating gift we can offer anyone, especially our children.

Most families are struggling.

Since 9/11, we have been living in fear, and the pandemic added yet another level of anxiety. Many of us are scared and feel out of control. We are compelled to monitor as many things as possible. We micromanage our little biospheres because we have no idea what tragic event will unfold next. We're on alert for every disaster imaginable. Our blood pressure rises and falls with each breaking news announcement. Fear of the perceived dangers that are around us is all-consuming. We're especially freaked out when it comes to raising our children. I'm here to say that it's okay to be scared now and then – parenting is hard work, but living in fear is not ok. We lose out on too many beautiful milestones in our children's lives when we're crippled by angst about their health and well-being. And living in a state of panic can also severely affect our health and well-being. Rates of anxiety, depression, and substance use are rising among parents – especially after the pandemic. We need to slow down, look around, and ask ourselves whether we are overacting.

In general, parents are inclined to fear things they can't control. We also tend to be particularly afraid of lurid and sensational hazards, those that draw media attention and make for movie-of-the-week melodramas. Dr. Alfred Sacchetti, a spokesman for the American College of Emergency Physicians, says it's common for parents to worry more about their child being abducted by a stranger than about them riding in a car without a seat belt or playing near an ungated swimming pool — even though car- and water-related accidents pose a far greater threat to kids than abduction. Unfortunately, much of what we're exposed to on TV is designed to generate ratings rather than educate parents. Our access to information doesn't keep up with our access to entertainment.

Recent studies have shown that many parents' fears are unfounded and frankly out of the scope of reality. I was shocked to learn that the top fear of American parents today is that their children won't get the education and opportunities they need to reach their potential. Pamela

Paul, the author of the book *Parenting Inc.,* has spent years examining the enormous baby-products marketing machine. In the book, Paul shows how parental anxiety fuels this lucrative industry. Marketers feed the fear, claiming educational toys and products and early reading programs will put kids on the fast track to success — before they're even out of diapers. Paul believes this parental anxiety is a rational reaction to a scary economic climate.

Parents are afraid that their children won't have an easy go of it because *they* aren't having an easy go of it. Many parents today are struggling to make ends meet and want a different kind of future for their kids. There's no question that we are living in a time of economic uncertainty. The cost of living is definitely on the rise, and, at the same time, wages are stagnant, and many jobs are being outsourced to foreign countries. It makes sense that parents are concerned about their children and how they'll fare in an increasingly competitive world. But this doesn't mean they should panic and begin grooming their child for college the day they're born. When it comes to helping your child reach their potential, it turns out that less is often more.

According to Paul, the average American child gets 70 new toys a year. We buy all these stimulants because we think it's helping our kids, but the fact is, creative kids need fewer toys. The kids with less are forced to use their imaginations, which helps them adjust to real life. Psychologist Paul Donahue, author of the book *Parenting Without Fear,* offers a similar perspective. He says parents think they should do it all for their kids: stimulate them, keep them constantly entertained, and do everything for them so they won't have to endure any frustration. They worry their child will fall behind if they don't assist them through challenging experiences. He argues that the reverse is actually true: Constant parental hovering makes it difficult for kids to develop independence, resourcefulness, imagination, and basic life skills — all things that will help a child perform well in school and life.

A few years back, I spearheaded an initiative in my hometown called Safe Routes to School. It is a program that helps make walking and biking to school safer and encourages kids to travel to school on foot or on their bikes. Our Home and School Associations started annual walk/bike to school months. We put together competitions, awarded prizes, and gave incentives. We did everything we could to help our community take advantage of our walkable town. But still, many parents chose to continue driving their kids to school – and in some cases, students were driven two or three blocks. This flummoxed me, so we conducted a comprehensive survey to determine the barriers to walking and biking.

I was stunned to learn that parents overwhelmingly feared stranger danger. It didn't make sense. We live in an affluent community outside New York City, where the chance of becoming a victim of a crime is meager, and certainly, nothing close to an abduction has ever occurred here. After doing some research, I found that it is not surprising that this is a top fear. There are few things as awful to contemplate as your child being hurt in a random attack. Those fears intensify because actual attacks on children get a lot of attention in the media, making them seem more common. Abductions by strangers are incredibly rare. Statistically, children are more likely to be struck by lightning than to be abducted by a stranger. I find parents' irrational fears about walking and biking to school very confusing, especially given the strong desire for their kids to perform well academically. Dr. John Ratey, an Associate Professor at Harvard Medical School, has done massive research on the connection between physical movement and brain function. His book, *Spark,* spells out why and how a brisk walk every morning helps us learn and retain more information. We shared this research with our community, yet parents still insist on driving their kids to school.

Rational fears for parents are accidents and injuries. I remember buying our kids a trampoline and watching them play. They had multiple close calls. It was terrifying for me. I worried about broken bones, sprained ankles, and the like, but fortunately, none of that happened. They ended up in the emergency room several times with other maladies, but that's what comes with growing up. The threat of accidents and injury among children is real, but they usually get hurt doing ordinary things like walking down the stairs or getting out of the bathtub. Hence, parents waste a lot of precious time worrying about catastrophes.

A reasonable concern for parents is bullying. Many of us worry that our children won't fit in socially and will be picked on. It's a fear that is impossible to dismiss since bullying is widespread among American schoolchildren. About 1 in 7 students in kindergarten through high school has either been a bully or a victim of bullying. Bullying should always be taken seriously, experts say, because it's been linked to long-term self-esteem issues, poor school performance, depression, and even suicide. Recent history also demonstrates that bullying can have widespread effects. It turns out that bullying operates like a virus: The worst bullies are often children who've been bullied themselves. Studies indicate that school shootings in recent years were perpetrated by kids who'd been bullied. Most school districts around the country have introduced anti-bullying programs to help educate children, teachers, and parents about recognizing and preventing bullying behaviors.

The motivations behind harmful bullying behavior can often be tricky to pinpoint. It can sometimes be a combination of things, so it's best to keep an open mind when trying to understand why a person might be using behaviors that appear to be bullying. There might be other things going on for them. Experts say children who experience violence at home are more apt to bully others, so this is yet another reason why it's crucial to never treat your child violently or allow others to do so. Parents lead by example. Our behaviors need to be in-check because more is caught than taught when raising kids. We must be proactive and teach our children from a young age that they shouldn't tease, call people names, or hurt others. If your child is a bully, take this behavior seriously. Initiate regular discussions with them about how they treat others and how to handle bullying if they experience or observe it. You should also help your child develop the resiliency and skills they need to protect themselves. Talk to your child about ways to respond to bullying, and even practice scripts they can use when and if they encounter bullying. Teach them how to build a kinder society by showing them that our differences make us unique and special and that our vulnerabilities are not weaknesses.

We want to shield our children as much as possible, but we've protected them so much that we're paralyzing them and, at the same time, redesigning society. My friend Lenore Skenazy is the president of Let Grow, a non-profit promoting childhood independence and resilience. Lenore is also the author of the book *Free Range Kids* and was the host of a television series called "World's Worst Mom." She is dedicated to helping parents and has spent the better part of her career encouraging us to let kids be kids. You should read her hilarious book whether your children are young or grown adults. You'll recognize yourself in its pages and learn to laugh at some of the absurd things we fret about. Of course, Lenore is all about safety, but she also has a comical way of reminding us that our kids don't need a security detail every time they go outside.

Kids are smarter and stronger than our culture gives them credit for. As parents, we must let our kids prove that to themselves and us. In the documentary "Chasing Childhood," Lenore says, "All the worry in the world doesn't prevent death; it prevents life!" I agree with her wholeheartedly. I'm not shaming people for hovering over their kids; I am validating them. The United States has been in a state of panic for 20+ years. My generation (Gen X) didn't grow up during wartime, so we're an especially freaked-out group. Before 9/11, we had no idea what evil looked like. Now we see it everywhere, whether it exists or not. The shocking truth is that we're living in some of the safest times in history, yet we behave like there is danger at every turn. Not only are we uneasy about the things that could happen to our offspring, but we also have the constant barrage of social media knocking on our conscience. We're comparing ourselves to every person in the world now. We measure our lives to their highlight reels, adding more anxiety to our already hectic lives. At some point, we need to let go of this angst and exhale because, guess what happens when we stop worrying? We are happy, and so are our kids. My friend and author Dr. Karen Latimer, a family physician and mother of five, says, "Parents everywhere hear this: You can calm down, take a breath, stop worrying, and do more for your kids by doing less. They will survive, thrive, and later thank you for giving them freedom. And you'll enjoy raising them in a happier, more peaceful home." In her Audible Original book *Take Back the House,* Dr. Latimer offers some down-home parenting advice for those ready to parent with more confidence and joy and encourages parents to be perfectly happy with imperfection. Every parent should take the time to listen to Dr. Latimer's book because it offers tips to gain peace of mind, a much-needed commodity when raising kids.

Here's the thing. Most of us spend excessive time unnecessarily worrying about the calamities our children may or may not experience. Doing so leaves us with a lot less time to focus on the most critical relationship in the family. And that is the bond that we have with our spouses. If we are genuinely committed to doing what is best for our kids, we need to be less focused on them and more focused on our marriage. Most people get married because they want a lasting relationship of love, friendship, and emotional intimacy. Achieving that marital ideal takes time, attention, and vigilance. Once kids come along, the effort and energy that goes into nurturing our marriage shifts and goes into caring for our kids; as a result, our marriage can become less satisfying.

When we had our first child, my husband and I were determined to be good parents. We responded to our daughter's cries quickly and consistently and with as much wisdom as first-time parents could muster. For a season, and rightfully so, we altered our lifestyle to accommodate her needs. We were always nearby, and we didn't worry about spoiling her. Both of us poured our hearts into nurturing our sweet little girl. It was rewarding and exhausting. Because we moved to San Antonio, Texas, just before she was born, we didn't have a support network, so after a year of sorting things out on our own, we finally signed up for a parenting class. It was a serious commitment. We attended the course three times a week for twenty-one weeks. You might think we are the world's best parents now, but you'd be wrong.

Some things stuck, but much fell by the wayside. The biggest takeaway from that experience has stayed with us, though, and I'm grateful. We learned that a child-centered marriage isn't good for anyone. Research confirms it. Studies show that marital satisfaction significantly plummets after the arrival of children and remains low during the child-rearing stages. No one tells us that, and more importantly, no one tells us what we can do about it. Couples acquiesce to their new way of life. They don't share what they are feeling, which is usually a mix of loneliness, feeling unappreciated, being pissed off at each other, and wondering where in the hell their sex life went.

Raising a family is a soul-shaping, relationship-altering experience; no marriage is ever the same once children come into the picture. Obviously, our kids bring us incredible joy, and as parents, we want to do everything we can to make them happy. But robbing your spouse of attention can be extremely detrimental to the family, so moving from a child-centered to a marriage-focused family helps everyone thrive. Regularly spending time alone with your mate and away from the kids is critical to a healthy family. Your partner needs to know they are valued and that your relationship is still a top priority. It sounds funny, but time spent not being a parent can actually make you better parents. It unifies and solidifies your mission to do what's best for the entire household. Plus, a romantic night out or quiet time alone can fulfill your human needs, wants, and goals outside of being a mom or dad. Spending time alone with your spouse helps create well-adjusted children too. Kids learn that their parents are unique individuals with their own interests and needs. When they see their parents interacting, they understand that they are separate from that union. They become less reliant on you and begin doing more things independently. Kids look to their parents as role models and will remember how you behaved when they grow up. Whether consciously or subconsciously, your behaviors translate to them, and if you do things right they will likely follow your lead and take better care of themselves when they're adults.

Setting a good example for your children now will last for generations. So make your marriage a priority. Find time to catch up with one another at the end of every day. Listen to your partner's problems and support them. Get in bed together at night and allow some time to touch, cuddle, talk, and reflect. And never forget that physical intimacy is incredibly important in a satisfying relationship. Don't ever stop courting and find ways to have new experiences together. Have a weekly date night or, better yet, schedule a weekend getaway. Eat, sleep in, have sex, watch movies, and go on adventures. Do what you used to do as a couple before the kids arrived. Repeat this often and remember the relationship you're building with your mate will remain when the kids leave the nest, so make it a good one!

Of course, lending individual-focused attention to our children and spouse is crucial to a happy and healthy household, but so is family time. I grew up in a family that was splintered. My parents had a rocky relationship, and my dad was often out of town for weeks, sometimes months at a time. I was the youngest of four children, and two of my older siblings were out of the house by the time I was ten. We spent time together during the holidays, but rarely, if ever, did we sit down and share a daily family meal. Because of all the upheaval, I spent a great deal of time at my aunty and uncle's home. The thing I enjoyed the most about being there was supper time. We all sat around their farmhouse table, ate, talked, and laughed. We enjoyed the meal because we all helped prepare it. My cousins would set the table, and when we were done, I would clean up and wash the dishes – by hand.

I felt so connected to them that I could cry now, remembering the love and warmth those experiences brought me. It was such a pivotal part of my childhood that I vowed to repeat it when I had my own family. So, with very few exceptions, my family and I sat down every night at 6 pm to a home-cooked meal. The kids would often help me prepare it, and they took turns setting the table or cleaning up the dishes. During dinner, we'd talk about the fun and unexpected things they experienced during the day, make plans for wild adventures, and discuss our dreams for the future. The kids are out of the house now, but both remember dinner hour as a bonding and valued experience.

As they were growing up, we shared lots of fond experiences with our kids, like playing Dominos, board games, and putting puzzles together. We spent many hours laughing and having fun together, gathered around a table. We'd often invite friends to join us, and we'd all have a great time. The kids are grown now, and we still engage in these activities. It's a family tradition that was taught to us by their grammy. These memories will sustain us through the rest of our lives. When we look back, simple experiences mean the most. Sure, we've had beautiful adventures traveling, going to the theater, parades, zoos, aquariums, etc., but nothing had the positive impact as our at-home family time did.

The time we invest in our family cannot be discounted. Studies have shown that spending time with family can help reduce stress and anxiety, lead to healthier lifestyles, and even lengthen life expectancy. Family time is key to a person's development because it promotes adaptability and resilience. These important lessons can only be taught by family members who lovingly coach us through life's ups and downs. Family time is what makes us who we are. Studies show that kids who spend quality time with their parents and siblings also tend to do better in school. They learn communication skills and the importance of education and can also get assistance with school assignments and new concepts when needed. This support reinforces that we are important to each other and that our success is valued in the family. Children who spend quality time with their families have shown less risk of behavioral issues and substance abuse. Receiving positive attention for positive behaviors increases our desire to continue healthy patterns. Being with family and doing activities together also provides an outlet for pent-up emotions that could otherwise lead to unhealthy decisions.

When it comes to needing advice, there is no better place to get it than from people who love you unconditionally. A loving family allows us to cope better with challenges and can significantly build personal confidence for all its members. That self-assuredness grows simply with knowing that we are valued and appreciated by our loved ones. Spending time with our family is fun, but it can be tricky too. When conflict arises, you can't just walk away for good. You're in this together, so you have to work together to solve issues. Our families teach interpersonal communication skills, including healthy, constructive ways to discuss, debate, and solve problems. Those with strong, healthy relationships tend to seek more beneficial coping mechanisms for stress, such as confiding in friends and family, instead of other unhealthy outlets like drinking and drug use. Establishing the habit of talking through problems and finding practical solutions helps everyone. A strong family bond dramatically improves the ability to face life's changes and challenges. Being with family gives us the feeling that we belong are cared for and are needed. It helps give us a sense of meaning and purpose in our lives. This assurance motivates us to push forward, grow and succeed. Spending time with family can also positively impact physical well-being with the right activities. For instance, participating in outdoor activities like sports games, hikes, or gardening helps improve fitness. There's evidence that family time can boost the effects of exercise and other healthy habits. It improves heart, brain, hormonal, and immune health. Being with family can also encourage one another to maintain healthy lifestyles. Healthy relationships could increase your lifespan by up to 50%. Combine all the physical and mental health benefits discussed above, and you can see why family ties have been linked to living a longer, healthier, and happier life. Even those with unhealthy physical habits but strong family bonds can live longer than those without these relationships.

CHAPTER TWO

Initiating Change

*"When you change the way you look at things,
the things you look at change."*
~ Wayne Dyer

The latest election seasons, the pandemic, and their aftermaths fractured our country in ways one could never imagine. I believe it's because we stopped communicating with one another. We don't listen as well as we used to and are hesitant to share our thoughts like we used to. We have our ideology and political beliefs, and most of us have decided that our way is the only way. When someone disagrees, many of us do not offer the courtesy of conversing because something negative has been pinched inside us. We have physical reactions to opposing views. We try to spare ourselves these uncomfortable feelings, so we decide not to talk to one another at all. This response furthers the breakdown of our families and society. When we assume that people with opposite views are not as well-read or intelligent as we are, it's impossible to learn from one another. And when we fail to offer generous assumptions about one another, we fail as a nation. We've been through a hell of a ride politically in the last decade. It's taken a toll on everyone, whether we're paying attention or not. Knowing that the divide we are experiencing may be due, in part, to our own feelings of fear and misperceptions about others and seeing that political leaders can inflame those thoughts and feelings gives us the ability to better understand how we've gotten to where we are. But there is a lot of work to be done to bring people together. Concentrating on face-to-face, mutually respectful, and curious conversations can work, even in seemingly hopeless situations. I fervently believe that we can reconnect our country and move forward together if we listen to and learn from one another, creating a better, safer world for our children and ourselves. But it takes effort and patience, and we all need to practice being better at communicating effectively.

Shortly after our 45th President's Inauguration, I helped organize a community-wide conversation in my hometown. It was an attempt to engage the enraged and help us all find common ground. We had the good fortune of hosting three national television personalities; Guy Benson, Julie Roginsky, and Lisa Kennedy. Guy is a conservative political analyst, Julie is a liberal political expert, and Kennedy is an independent. When I introduced the panel, I said, "My goal for the evening is to help us step out of our red and blue bubbles and move toward the purple center. The way to do this is through generous listening. That means putting down our preconceived ideas and genuinely listening to those with opposing views. If we are to make kind-hearted assumptions, we need to believe that while we may differ in opinion, we have all done some research, and we've just interpreted information differently. We can find common ground more easily if we start there." I placed printed conversation prompts on the tables and encouraged the audience to start dialogs with their tablemates. I urged participants to discuss these neutral topics, listen attentively to one another, and then take the conversation to a deeper level by making brief comments during the exchange. The phrases I suggested were "Help me understand." and "Tell me more." The discussions were simple – What is your favorite cookie and why? Where is your favorite place in town to go for a walk? When these uncomplicated subjects were discussed, people learned how to turn down their protective covers and open up their hearts. We learned that Joe liked oatmeal raisin cookies because his mother baked them for him when he was a little boy, making him feel loved. We learned that Janis likes to walk near the brook because the sound of the water helps her feel less anxiety and more peace. Taking the time to say "help me understand" and "tell me more" can change a conversation's entire direction. When people are asked in a respectful way to explain their positions, highly charged conversations can be defused, and quality information can be exchanged. When we genuinely care about and listen to people, deeper and more meaningful connections are made. Meaningful conversations include generous listening, compassion, and tolerance. When we slow down and take time to engage in thoughtful dialog, empathy and patience become visible, and humanity wins. This approach is the way to heal our country, this is the way to heal families, and honestly, it is how we heal ourselves.

Getting the Help We Need

I explained earlier in the book about a marriage retreat my husband and I attended a few years ago called "Getting the Love You Want: A Guide for Couples." Top relationship experts Drs. Harville Hendrix and Helen LaKelly Hunt facilitated it. They believe that how we interact with each other in all our contexts—family, workplace, schools, etc.—is the key to our emotional, physical, and economic well-being and the well-being of our children and society. They envision the possibility of shifting from the age of the individual to the age of the relationship when "relationship" rather than the "individual" will be the primary value system of culture. They co-initiated Imago Relationship Therapy. The program is designed for couples and families, but Hendrix and LaKelly Hunt recognized that the techniques they teach could also be helpful in our broader society. So they launched a powerful program called Relationships First.

Working with community organizations such as schools, churches, police departments, and first responders, Hendrix and LaKelly Hunt show people how to connect and communicate effectively, despite differences, using a three-step process called "Safe Conversations," a program that helps people from all walks of life and backgrounds become more compassionate and mindful in their relationships. The system is almost identical to Imago Relationship Therapy. It teaches people to talk without criticism, listen without judgment, and connect beyond differences. And as in IRT the key concepts are mirroring, validating, and empathizing. When having a safe conversation, your conversation partner is to reflect back word-for-word what you have expressed.

The purpose is to deeply understand what was said and confirm that it has been heard and received. The first part of a safe conversation is to ask permission to have a meaningful dialog. When all parties agree, the person on the listening end of the exchange must validate what is being expressed by the speaker and verify that they understand the speaker's point of view. They don't necessarily have to agree with it, but they must continue asking questions until they fully comprehend the opinion or point of view. What follows is empathizing. The listener puts themselves in the speaker's shoes and imagines what it must feel like to have experienced the story they shared. The listener continues asking, "Is there anything else?" until the speaker fully communicates their feelings. The overwhelming success of the relationships first program proves that finding common ground beyond our differences is possible when we learn to express them without disapproval and listen without condemnation. We all want to be seen and heard, and this technique helps people get the validation they inherently desire as human beings. Communication is equally important. When the focus is on alignment rather than agreement or disagreement, we can realize higher levels of satisfaction, cooperation, and collaboration in all our relationships.

If you find yourself in a setting where opinions clash or you disagree with someone, try being vulnerable enough to come to an alignment. Give the safe conversations technique a try, and keep in mind that vulnerability is not a sign of weakness but a sure path to more meaningful conversations and profound connections. Ask permission to have an honest discussion. Paraphrase your understanding of the issue from the other person's perspective to ensure clarity. Finally, offer truthful, compassionate feedback and always remember that we all share the exact needs; they are to be seen and heard.

Other movements have recently popped up to help Americans communicate more effectively and bridge the partisan divide. Braver Angels is one example. Braver Angels got its start using marriage counseling techniques to bring Republicans and Democrats together. Their goal is to positively impact community life and American institutions, specifically grassroots organizations, academia, the media, politics, and government. The foundation of their activities is what they refer to as "patriotic empathy." The idea is for Americans to express love for our country by showing concern for our fellow citizens and not a particular political figure or party.

The approach is to communicate respectfully through various means and try to understand the other side's point of view. The Braver Angel program encourages people to engage with those they disagree with, look for simple ways to work together, and support principles that bring us together rather than divide us. They have multiple platforms that assist in accomplishing these goals. I've been on several calls that have connected people from across the country to discuss a range of issues. The facilitators emphasize storytelling, listening, and learning, rather than declaring or debating. They encourage people to share and learn and not lecture or give feedback about how to think or say things differently. Participants take turns responding to a series of questions while people listen without cross-talk. People take turns sharing what they've learned regarding others' views and experiences, and they try to find common ground. The exchanges close after parties devise an action plan that can make a positive difference. When the formal conversation ends, participants are encouraged to speak to one another in an unstructured dialog. This allows them to dig deeper into issues, ask opinions about current events and keep up with personal information such as family, jobs, etc. The program is expanding its reach daily and is a successful initiative that we can turn to in an effort to learn better ways of talking about serious issues affecting our daily lives. The most critical function of the Braver Angel technique is listening to understand; as we're learning, that is the only thing that will bring us closer together.

Another wonderful organization that focuses on effective communication is the Compassionate Listening Project. It is one of the oldest organizations in the world engaged in people-to-people peace mediation. It started in the early nineties when a group of deeply informed and caring individuals traveled to the Middle East to teach reconciliation skills. In the last three decades, they have taken hundreds of American citizens to Israel and Palestine to listen to and learn about the grievances, hopes, and dreams of people on both sides of that conflict. Religious, political, and grassroots leaders, refugees, peace activists, citizens, soldiers, and extremists attend workshops to find ways to strengthen support for peace. As that mission continues, leaders from the Compassionate Listening Project have created a curriculum to teach peace-building skills to average people living everyday lives. The trainings and workshop journeys are offered worldwide, in person, and remotely throughout the year. The demand for compassionate listening training in the U.S. has dramatically increased in recent years, so workshops are now available to academia, churches, jails, and other public and private settings. The sessions are appropriately named "Compassionate Listening – Healing Our World from the Inside Out" because they help communities learn about cross-cultural and interfaith issues and give lessons on human rights and humanitarian work.

We all know that our country suffers from deep racial tensions and increasing political polarization. But we can do something about it using the Compassionate Listening Project tools. The core practices of compassionate listening are cultivating compassion and respect for oneself and others, suspending judgment, and listening with and speaking from the heart. These principles can assist us in sincere self-reflection about our conscious and unconscious biases and help us cause less harm in our relationships. Implementing these ideas can help melt our fearful hearts, enhance understanding, heal divisions, and turn former enemies into partners for peace.

The goal of this book is to help spouses, parents, leaders, followers, and everyone in between become better communicators. Effective communicators are trusted individuals who people typically turn to for advice because they listen deeply, speak honestly, and demonstrate that they value others. These are the people who simplify complex topics and break down information in a way that helps everyone understand. They express their ideas and opinions freely and understand the importance of being direct while remaining respectful if they disagree with others. Good conversationalists have a unique style that's all their own. They infuse humor and personal stories to keep listeners engaged but, more importantly, they listen to understand and validate the other's thoughts. Validation is a simple concept to understand but challenging to put into practice. When someone expresses it, it is powerful because you can see yourself and your thoughts reflected. Your values, patterns, and choices are highlighted.

Hearing that someone appreciates our points of view and understands where we're coming from can calm our fears and concerns and can add joy and excitement to our conversations. Being around effective communicators helps us feel empowered and ready to take big risks because we know someone is in our corner. Who doesn't want to be a person like this? When we're in the company of people who care about us, we start to care more about ourselves and often give more freely to others, and, most importantly, we begin to believe that anything is possible and that all our dreams can come true. Imagine the power and freedom we can all feel by learning to communicate effectively. When we take time to consider it, we realize that every person on the planet has value, and everyone is a treasured contributor to society. Some make indelible contributions through science, art, and technology, and their gifts are remembered in tangible ways. But all of us can positively influence society simply by empowering others through communicating effectively, listening with compassion, and giving to others with care. Ordinary people like you and me can impact our families, communities, and, yes, the world just by taking time to listen to others with our whole hearts. Hence, this book is dedicated to helping people everywhere become wholehearted listeners.

The guidelines on these pages are designed to help you learn more about who you are so you can offer empathy, understanding, and compassion to yourself and others. The goal, dear reader, is for you to learn how to set aside time for honest conversation and devote your thoughts to what your mind, body, and spirit are telling you so you can give full attention to yourself and the people around you. Wholehearted listening doesn't come naturally to any of us; it requires a lot of love and effort. Listening with our heart requires us to know ourselves enough to keep our thoughts to ourselves and refrain from interrupting and saying things that will make the speaker feel invisible. It requires us to get past our defensiveness when we don't want to hear what the other person is saying and leave space for their anger and pain. The capacity for intimacy and connection is directly proportional to our ability to develop these connections with others.

Sometimes we forget that our most important relationship is with ourselves. We need to give ourselves the time and space to understand our internal dialog clearly. Our most authentic communication originates from the heart through intuition, not reasoning or logical assumptions. So don't try to rationalize your thoughts. Instead, recognize the importance of getting to know yourself and the significance of honest reflection. Setting aside time for this will help you be more empathetic to the needs and issues your heart is pointing toward. If you can't show empathy and support for yourself first, chances are you will not be able to offer compassion and support to anyone else. Life is short, which is why it is so important to enjoy every single moment. It's easy to lose sight of the big picture, so take time every day to evaluate the things that matter the most to you and pay attention to all the things you can be grateful for. All of this looks and feels different for everyone, but one thing remains the same: opportunities abound for all of us. Nobody wants to live with regret, so if you want a change, take a reasonable approach and dive into it. You can't afford to miss out on all the extraordinary things that await you. Modern society wants us to take life super seriously. But my suggestion is not to let yourself fall into that trap. It's better to be positive, laugh more, and relax into your struggles. There is freedom in accepting things as they are and finding the good amidst the bad. You are the author of your life story, so don't follow the crowd or turn your power over to anyone else. Follow your heart and make decisions from that unique place. And remember to take good care of yourself. Creating daily self-care rituals helps us love and nurture ourselves, and it helps us feel in balance with the universe. Ultimately, all that matters is that you can look in the mirror every day and be proud of the image that is staring back at you. That's true happiness. We can't take all of our problems away, but we can wake up every day with a grateful heart. Everyone can turn a negative situation into a positive one, and it is our right as human beings to live the life we love. In the words of poet A.R. Lucas, "If there's even a slight chance at getting something that will make you happy, risk it. Life's too short, and happiness is too rare."

CHAPTER THREE

LEAD

*"Love your life, empower others,
act on opportunity, and do good!"*
~ Jeanne Hope Johnson

T his book is designed to help us be better leaders by being better listeners. When we listen to ourselves, we heal ourselves, our families, and our society. In this next section of the book, we will take a deep dive into the LEAD system. It's something I dreamed up on a flight home from Austin a few years ago. I had spent a long weekend with some terrific friends who were starting a boutique management consulting firm. The three of us brainstormed concepts for days. The LEAD system came to mind, and we agreed it is a straightforward and easy-to-understand approach to conducting ourselves in business and our personal lives.

Love Your Life

Look around. All kinds of things can bring you joy and peace. If something is amiss, listen to your body, mind, and soul and let their messages help you understand and meet your needs. When your needs are fulfilled, you will have more clarity and confidence to pursue your goals, engage in meaningful relationships, and navigate life's challenges with resilience and purpose.

Empower Others

You have more influence than you realize. Every interaction, decision, and expression of your values has a ripple effect on the people and the world around you. Recognizing and harnessing this influence allows you to impact and inspire others positively. Embracing your ability to influence means taking responsibility for the energy you bring into different situations. By understanding the power of your words and actions, you can cultivate a positive environment and encourage those around you to reach their full potential. Embrace your influence, and you'll find opportunities to lead, inspire, and shape better, more connected relationships.

Act on Opportunity

Opportunities are everywhere, but we often don't notice them because we're too busy, not paying attention, or not expecting them. Improving your listening skills and trusting your instincts can help you discover "lucky breaks."

Do Good

Contributing good for the benefit of others generates a cycle of kindness. Meaningful work changes us and helps families and communities bond in beautiful ways.

Love Your Life

"This above all. To thine own self, be true."
~ Shakespeare

I have learned that it is challenging to influence others unless I honestly understand myself and my intentions. How can I make a difference to someone when I can't figure myself out? This section is about getting to know yourself better so you can feel good about who you are and your impact on others.

Quick Quiz

The quiz below is an easy way to gauge if you truly know yourself. Answer the five questions on a scale of 1 to 10.

1. Do you understand why you feel the way you do?

1   2   3   4   5   6   7   8   9   10

2. Do you know how you give and receive love?

1   2   3   4   5   6   7   8   9   10

3. Do you know what your purpose in life is?

1   2   3   4   5   6   7   8   9   10

4. Do you know your strengths and weaknesses and accept them?

1   2   3   4   5   6   7   8   9   10

5. If someone asked, "Who are you?" would you be able to answer that question?

1   2   3   4   5   6   7   8   9   10

Now, add up your score. The closer it is to 50, the more you know yourself, the more comfortable you are with yourself, and the more significant your influence on the people around you.

Keep in mind this test is a teaser. You might feel pretty good about your score or be in a fog of wonder about why you scored so low. Don't let this simple quiz determine how well you know yourself because many more comprehensive personality profile tests are available to you. I encourage you to research them all and take one or two - or more. I feel like I've taken them all, and each one has given me deeper insights into why I do the things I do and why I am the way I am. These tests have helped highlight my strengths and weaknesses, which helps me a lot, especially when working with a team.

Each personality test has its strong points when it comes to examining how we're wired. Access to that kind of data helps bring us more self-awareness. The tests bring our core competencies and traits to light and can bring us much more self-fulfillment.

The first personality profile test I took years ago was the Myers-Briggs Type Indicator (MBTI). It is one of the first comprehensive "personality" tests formulated. It was introduced by Katharine Cook Briggs and her daughter, Isabel Briggs Myers, in the 1940s. The theory is that humans experience the world using four psychological functions: sensation, intuition, feeling, and thinking. These functions affect many things, such as one's work style, mode of rejuvenation, strengths, weaknesses, etc. It measures whether you are extroverted or introverted, what your intuitive preference is when it comes to processing information, whether you prefer to make decisions by thinking or feeling, and whether you have judging or perceiving preferences about how you do things.

No one personality type is "best" or "better" than another, and this test isn't a tool designed to look for dysfunction or abnormality. Instead, its goal is simply to help you learn more about yourself. The questionnaire itself is made up of four different scales.

Extraversion (E) – Introversion (I): The extraversion-introversion contrast is a way to describe how people respond and interact with the world around them. While these terms are familiar to most people, how they are used in the MBTI differs somewhat from their widespread usage.

Extroverts are "outward-turning" and tend to be action-oriented, enjoy more frequent social interaction, and feel energized after spending time with others. Introverts are "inward-turning" and are thought-oriented, enjoy deep and meaningful social interactions, and feel recharged after spending time alone. We all exhibit extraversion

41

and introversion to some degree, but most of us tend to prefer one or the other.

Sensing (S) – Intuition (N): This scale involves looking at how people gather information from the world around them. Just like extroversion and introversion, all people spend time sensing and intuiting depending on the situation. According to the MBTI, people tend to be dominant in one area or the other. People who prefer sensing tend to pay attention to reality, particularly to what they can learn from their own senses. They tend to focus on facts and details and enjoy getting hands-on experience. Those who prefer intuition pay more attention to things like patterns and impressions. They enjoy thinking about possibilities, imagining the future, and abstract theories.

Thinking (T) – Feeling (F): This scale focuses on how people make decisions based on the information that they gather from their sensing or intuition functions. People who prefer thinking place a greater emphasis on facts and objective data. They tend to be consistent, logical, and impersonal when weighing a decision. Those who prefer feeling are more likely to consider people and emotions when arriving at a conclusion.

Judging (J) – Perceiving (P): The final scale involves how people tend to deal with the outside world. Those who lean toward judging prefer structure and firm decisions. People who lean toward perceiving are more open, flexible, and adaptable. These two tendencies interact with the other scales.

Remember, all people spend some time engaged in extroverted activities. The judging-perceiving scale helps describe whether you behave like an extrovert when taking in new information (sensing and intuiting) or making decisions (thinking and feeling). Each type is then listed by its four-letter code:

ISTJ - The Inspector: Reserved and practical, they tend to be loyal, orderly, and traditional.

ISTP - The Crafter: Highly independent, they enjoy new experiences that provide first-hand learning.

ISFJ - The Protector: Warm-hearted and dedicated, they are always ready to protect the people they care about.

ISFP - The Artist: Easy-going and flexible, they tend to be reserved and artistic.

INFJ - The Advocate: Creative and analytical, they are considered one of the rarest Myers-Briggs types.[3]

INFP - The Mediator: Idealistic with high values, they strive to make the world a better place.

INTJ - The Architect: High logical, they are both very creative and analytical.[4]

INTP - The Thinker: Quiet and introverted, they are known for having a rich inner world.

ESTP - The Persuader: Outgoing and dramatic, they enjoy spending time with others and focusing on the here and now.

ESTJ - The Director: Assertive and rule-oriented; they have high principles and a tendency to take charge.

ESFP - The Performer: Outgoing and spontaneous, they enjoy taking center stage.

ESFJ - The Caregiver: Soft-hearted and outgoing, they tend to believe the best about others.

ENFP - The Champion: Charismatic and energetic, they enjoy situations where they can put their creativity to work.

ENFJ - The Giver: Loyal and sensitive, they are known for being understanding and generous.

ENTP - The Debater: Highly inventive, they love being surrounded by ideas and tend to start many projects (but may struggle to finish them).

ENTJ - The Commander: Outspoken and confident, they are great at making plans and organizing projects.

The Myers-Briggs Type Indicator is a popular instrument that can provide valuable insight into your personality. Even without taking the formal questionnaire, you can probably recognize some of your tendencies. It is important to remember that every type has its own unique value. For instance, when working in group situations at school or work, understanding your strengths and those of others can be extremely beneficial.

My boss asked our team to take the DiSC profile recently. It is a personal assessment tool used to help improve teamwork, communication, and productivity in the workplace. The model is based on four primary personality traits, each represented by a corresponding letter:

(D) Dominance: Individuals with a dominance style are often described as assertive, decisive, and results-oriented. They tend to focus on achieving goals, taking charge, and solving problems.

(I) Influence: Those with an influence style are often sociable, enthusiastic, and persuasive. They enjoy interacting with others and building relationships and are often skilled at inspiring and motivating people.

(S) Steadiness: Individuals with a steadiness style are typically calm, patient, and supportive. They value cooperation, harmony, and a stable environment. They are often good listeners and team players.

(C) Conscientiousness: Those with a conscientiousness style are detail-oriented, analytical, and systematic. They emphasize accuracy and thoroughness and prefer to work in a structured and organized manner.

Everyone is a blend of all four DiSC styles—usually, one, two, or even three types stand out. Each person has a unique behavioral profile with different styles and priorities—no one style is better or worse than the next. The DiSC assessment is useful because it can help you become more self-aware, and understanding your teammates' profiles can help you appreciate and understand their habits and motivations.

The Enneagram, Rorschach Inkblot, and True Colors tests are also helpful tools for becoming more self-aware. I've taken them all, and they all revealed about the same feedback. I sometimes wish I could change things about my personality, but as I get older, I have learned to accept who I am and play to my strengths. The world needs people like me. It needs you, too. So, consider taking a couple of these tests to discover more about yourself and how to increase your capacity to serve the people around you. Top of Form

Everything is better if we look at it from the inside out. The Pixar film with the same name, "Inside Out," is a delightful tale about how our emotions can control us if we let them. The animated movie focuses on Riley, a 15-year-old girl whose emotional core is shaken when she moves from Minnesota to San Francisco. Her five key emotions—Joy, Sadness, Anger, Fear, and Disgust—need to learn how to evolve to guide her through this pivotal life change. The movie offers valuable lessons about recognizing, respecting, validating, and processing complex emotions.

Handling our reactions in positive ways can be challenging, especially when world-shifting events like the COVID-19 pandemic and other heartbreaking tragedies make it harder to cope with a flood of feelings. To recognize how valuable our circumstances are, we need to do some self-examination to find out what makes us tick.

We all have core memories. They are the pivotal moments in our lives that have shaped us into the person we are today. These memories may be attached to a mix of emotions as we age. Or we may look back on them through rose-colored glasses. Either way, tapping into those recollections is important because they make us who we are.. Our memories remind us of the times we felt triumphant when we took a leap of faith or fueled our desire to fight for others, and they inform us about what we truly love, enjoy, or need to avoid for our mental and emotional well-being. Our memories help us recall that life hasn't been perfect, but we are capable, unique, and loved. To understand ourselves better, we must examine our memories and process the emotions we experienced during pivotal moments.

The Safe Conversation tools I mentioned earlier in the book can help you process through deep-seated memories. Acknowledging and validating our feelings from past incidents is cathartic and necessary. Often, we don't allow sadness to take up any space, but sometimes, that emotion can give us the best information. It is imprinted on our subconscious that we are always expected to be happy and take everything in stride, even during difficult transitions. We deal with the pressure to appear happy so we don't seem like a downer, preventing us from confronting our sadness. Messages of being "strong" and having "good vibes" seem to rule, and the encouragement to steer clear of sadness often starts in childhood. Grownups angrily tell kids to stop crying, even when they have a good reason to. That early messaging informs us that we cannot be openly sad because it makes others uncomfortable. Sadness doesn't feel pleasant, but it's a necessary emotion. We are human beings and have the right to experience a range of feelings. It *is* okay to cry. Sadness allows us to listen to ourselves and process our feelings instead of burying them for temporary comfort. If we try to ignore it, we are setting ourselves up for future pain and suffering. Sadness also taps into our empathetic core, gives us a needed release, and can help us view a situation with emotional clarity. Embrace sadness because emotions aren't good or bad, though we tend to categorize them as such. Joy is good, sadness is terrible, anger is destructive, and so on. We are typically taught to put on a brave face and respond to "How are you?" positively or neutrally and that the "good" emotions are the most important. In reality, feelings are what they are.

Marcia Reynolds, PsyD., addressed this in a *Psychology Today* piece about "bad" emotions. She says that all emotions are a part of our human experience. You can't experience joy without sorrow, peace without anger, and courage without fear. Life is richer when we allow ourselves the grace to move through the dark and the light. How we project our feelings into the world can lead to negative or positive interactions. For example, it's not okay to angrily lash out at someone who calls out a truth that makes you uncomfortable or upset. However, anger is productive in the face of injustice because it incites action and causes disenfranchised people and their allies to fight for what's right.

Anger can frequently give you positive drive and motivation. It's imperative to respect our emotional centers, acknowledge when we are feeling something, sit with that feeling, and make wise choices about how to engage with that emotion. Many expect us to be happy and go with the flow because that's "what we always do." But they should consider that we may have often feigned happiness to gain approval. But we have a right to be sad and angry. Those feelings are something we all share. Sometimes, we expect others to react in a way that is "sensible" from our perspective. Our experiences and privileges inform what triggers us, motivates us, and causes a shift from our norm. Even if we think we know someone well, we don't understand all the intricacies that lead to certain emotions controlling their brains. Each person has their own set of memories, some of which may be painful, sad, or anxiety-filled. Give yourself the room to feel what you feel.

We should all strive to give people space to embrace their emotions honestly, and they should do the same for us. Giving and receiving support helps us feel whole. These moments teach us to cope with the truth and accept things as they are. With support from friends and loved ones, we can better move sadness into the back seat and move forward with joy.

We must remind ourselves to embrace all our emotions and permit ourselves not to be "okay." We must also allow those around us to work through their emotional realizations. It's not about avoiding uncomfortable feelings but rather going towards them to get honest with ourselves and grow. Emotions play an essential role in how we think and behave. The emotions we feel each day can compel us to take action and influence the decisions we make about our life, both large and small. Feelings can be short-lived, a flash of annoyance at a friend or co-worker, or long-lasting, such as sadness over the loss of a relationship. Emotions influence our decisions, from what we have for breakfast to which candidates we choose to vote for in political elections. While evidence suggests that some feelings are universal, no one-size-fits-all emotional balance suits every culture or individual.

If I feel anxious about something, haven't budgeted my time well, or am distracted, I cannot focus on the good things in life. When I'm in that frame of mind, influencing anyone positively, especially myself, is almost impossible. It's even more difficult if I am experiencing negative feelings toward something or someone. Thankfully, I've recognized that I don't have to be a perfect person to do good things, and neither do you. If we're honest about our feelings, we can admit we are frustrated, angry, or upset. We can authentically communicate these things to the people around us and move on. We can "feel the feels," but we shouldn't stay in that place long because bigger and better things need to be experienced. It's not okay to pretend that all is well, but putting negative feelings aside is a good idea until you have the proper time to focus on processing them. When we don't acknowledge our uncomfortable emotions, the result is called "toxic positivity." It means we deny and suppress what we're feeling. Toxic positivity tells us that the emotion we are feeling is wrong and shouldn't exist; if we try just a little bit harder, we can eliminate it. That is an unhealthy practice.

On the other hand, when we acknowledge and accept our emotions, we can experience them fully and not run from them. This helps us move into a place of authentic optimism. It's not easy to fully process every feeling, but it's worth the effort. If it's too painful, then the most efficient thing you can do to get out of a low mental space is to stop focusing on yourself and start focusing on being grateful for the good things in your life. No one can be angry and grateful simultaneously, so concentrate on joy, and you'll see that your attitude will quickly change, and you'll feel better about almost everything. It is important to remember that we have three parts when understanding ourselves. We have our physical body, mind, and spirit.

Each plays an essential role in managing life's ups and downs. In the next section, you will learn how to listen to each part of yourself to maintain a positive attitude. Listening to your body is critical. Using a combination of self-care and self-awareness helps us maintain a life of contentment. One of the tools that I've used for years is the HALT technique. This handy acronym reminds us to take a moment (HALT) and ask ourselves if we are feeling **H**ungry, **A**ngry, **L**onely, or **T**ired. It seems simple enough, but we are susceptible to self-destructive behaviors when these basic needs are unmet. Fortunately, hunger, anger, loneliness, and tiredness are easy to address and serve as a warning system before things reach a breaking point.

Hunger can be a physical or emotional need. Understanding the need to eat is pretty straightforward. However, we should remind ourselves not just to eat but to eat well. Meeting nutritional needs allows our bodies to operate at their highest potential. However, when we HALT and assess our situation, we can describe a hunger for less tangible things such as affection, accomplishment, and understanding. Give thought to your emotions and share your feelings with people who care about and love you. They will give you food for your heart and help ease the emotional hunger that you're feeling.

Anger, as we pointed out earlier, is a normal, healthy emotion. It is important to HALT and take time to understand what is causing your anger and know how to express it appropriately. Maybe you're angry with a situation, a person, or yourself. It might be a little thing that spins out of control, or an ongoing event. No matter what is bothering you, assess whether or not you can confront it. Calmly talk to the person you have an issue with to fix the problem. If what is angering you is out of your control, or you aren't ready to confront the case, try to express yourself in other ways. Exercising, punching a pillow, or even cleaning the house are active ways to eliminate the excess energy anger brings. Creative projects such as painting, singing, or writing might be a better way for you to dispel your anger. Meditation or prayer can also be a way to calm yourself anywhere and at any time. Finally, talking to someone who isn't involved in the situation can be beneficial to think through your anger. Regardless of how you dismiss your anger, acknowledge it and reflect upon its causes so you can release it in constructive, not destructive, ways.

Loneliness can occur when we are alone or surrounded by many people. We isolate ourselves when we feel like others don't understand us. We withdraw into ourselves out of fear and doubt. Being alone is a self-imposed situation. If you're feeling lonely, HALT and ask yourself if you have reached out to anyone lately. Your support system is there for you when you feel depressed, overwhelmed, anxious, or need someone to talk to. Calling a friend or visiting a loved one might be just what you need. You can also walk, run errands, or go to a coffee shop. Rather than hiding from everyone, connect with others who want to see you happy and healthy.

Tiredness takes a toll on our body, mind, and spirit. Ignoring how weary we become when our days are filled with tasks, meetings, and activities is easy. However, running on low energy compromises our ability to think and our capacity to cope. Taking the time to HALT is particularly important when you're tired. Satisfying the physical need to sleep, rest, and rejuvenate is critical to keeping physically, emotionally, and spiritually healthy. A good night's sleep or a quick nap may be all you need to change your outlook for the day. Recharging your body, mind, and spirit will help you get through challenging times.

Using the **HALT** acronym reminds us to take care of our basic needs daily. Periodically take a moment to check in with yourself and ask, "Am I hungry, angry, lonely, or tired?" Honestly assessing how you feel takes only a minute, and doing so will make everyday stressors more manageable.

We all have different voices inside our heads, and often they're in conflict. Whether your inner voice is loud and clear or more of a whisper, tending to it can be a great source of guidance when you need it most. In terms of making big decisions (and sometimes even small ones), the three most important voices to discern are the voice of fear, the voice of reason, and the voice of intuition. The voice of fear comes from the body. It's a primal emotional fight-or-flight response that can be traced all the way back to the reptilian brain. Its job is to warn us of anything that might be dangerous or cause us pain.

While fear-based responses often seem irrational, they're actually *pre-rational*. Fear precedes reason. Fear has been around for hundreds of millions of years. Reason, however, is a relative newcomer to the party. The voice of reason comes from the mind, specifically from the neocortex, and is not emotional. It's a capacity for rational thought that analyzes pros and cons and makes sound decisions. Listening to your voice of reason provides comfort in knowing you have considered the facts of a situation and have given everyone involved the best you have to give. You have also shown your best self to others by remaining reasonably respectful and honest.

The voice of intuition comes from the spirit. Where the voice of fear is pre-rational, and the voice of reason is rational, the voice of intuition is *trans-rational*. It exists beyond reason. That's why it seldom shows up in the form of thoughts or ideas. Instead, it acts more like a GPS device, helping us determine whether our choices are on course or not. Where the voice of fear worries and the voice of reason analyzes, the voice of intuition resonates. Intuition is your gut reaction to thoughts and decisions. It either offers a distinctly positive sensation, or it goes thud. The voice of intuition shows up most commonly as a feeling of joy, excitement, purpose, or inspiration. For me, something that's "on course" lights me up —it pulls my awareness up toward my heart and fills me with a feeling of joy. When something is "off-course," I feel disconnected, pulling my awareness down toward my feet and leaving me feeling empty. And then some things don't seem to matter to the voice of intuition at all —they don't resonate one way or the other. Of the three voices, the voice of intuition is the surest guide to your highest good. It's the best advocate for your enlightened self-interest. It's a compass needle pointing directly toward your greatest joy.

The voice of intuition is always present, yet it can also be the most difficult voice to hear and the hardest voice to trust. Learning to listen to your inner dialog can be as simple as setting the daily intention to tap into it. You don't need much time for this, just three minutes a few times a day. Find a quiet space. Put your hand on your heart and close your eyes. Take a deep cleansing breath through your nose, and exhale for as long as you can through your mouth. Do this three times in a row. You will feel immediate relief, which will help you concentrate more clearly. You'll feel more relaxed and ready to face obstacles because your intuition will kick in.

Simply put, our inner voice is our innate intelligence and is the truth of our inner being. When we listen to it, we turn inward to hear what our body and soul are saying before looking to the world outside ourselves for direction. Allowing your inner voice to guide you can help you fully understand your wisdom, guidance, and purpose in life. There's nothing more potent than trusting yourself and confidently following your truth. It allows you to show up as the best version of yourself in all that you do. The bottom line is, whatever helps you get in touch with your inner voice, do it and do it often. It may seem easier to look for answers outside of yourself, but with patience, practice, trust, and good listening skills, you'll be able to tune into your authentic self for guidance when you need it most. But remember, your inner voice can turn to self-talk, which can sometimes be destructive, so be sure to say nice things to yourself. If you catch yourself polluting your mind, cut it out. Your mind holds thoughts, and thoughts can change if you want them to. It really is that simple, but it takes self-awareness to reframe your old way of thinking with a new and improved mindset. "Change your thoughts, and you change your world." This powerful quote by Norman Vincent Peale can be life-altering. Research unanimously agrees. From sports performance to losing weight to combatting depression, changing how you talk to yourself can have a proactive role in behavior changes. Consider using this *Listen, Learn and Think it Through* exercise to improve your self-talk.

Step One: Listen: Keep a diary for a few days to a week, and take it everywhere. Pay close attention to your self-talk and make a note of the following:

- Is it mostly positive or negative?

- What events, people, or scenarios encourage positive versus negative self-talk?

- What would a friend or loved one say if they knew you talked to yourself this way?

- Are there any common threads in your self-talk?

Step Two: Learn: At the end of the week, reflect on what you have written. Think about the following questions:

- What thoughts come up most often?

- Why do they come up?

- How would you feel about yourself if you switched negative self-talk to positive?

- How did negative self-talk hold you back from achieving your goals?

- What might you achieve if you practiced more positive self-talk?

Step Three: Think it Through. To move from negative to positive self-talk, you need to think over why you had the thoughts in the first place and answer honestly about how accurate these thoughts are. Here are a few questions to use for this final part of the exercise:

- How big of a deal is this? Might I be overreacting?

- Are my thoughts and conclusions based on facts or opinions? Whose opinions?

- Am I guessing at information and making assumptions?

- How accurate is this thought, really?

Now that you know where your negative self-talk might be holding you back, and when it arises, you can look to switch gears about how you talk to yourself. Here's a great follow-on exercise from *Listen, Learn and Think it Through*. The exercise involves taking the negative self-talk you use and reframing it with a positive self-talk alternative.

For example:

- Negative Self-Talk: 'I am such an idiot! I screwed up that project, and there's no coming back.'

Switch to

Positive Self-Talk: 'I didn't do as well as I know I can, but that's okay. Now I know what I can do next time to improve, which will help my personal and professional growth.'

- Negative Self-Talk: 'This deadline is impossible; I'll never be able to get the work done.'

Switch to

Positive Self-Talk: 'This is a lot to accomplish, and I can only do what I can. As long as I keep my colleagues/boss informed, I'm sure we can make this work.'

- Negative Self-Talk: 'What's the point in going? Everyone will see what an imposter I am.'

Switch to

Positive Self-Talk: 'Meeting new people can be daunting, but I'm a good person with lots to offer.'

Keep practicing and rehearsing how you switch up your negative self-talk; over time, you'll find that positive self-talk begins to come more naturally to you.

Listen to your spirit; it always tries to communicate something. Sometimes it's telling you to relax and take it easy. Other times it's guiding you on a path to your life mission in relationships or career. Your spirit has a unique and quiet way of speaking; sometimes, it comes to you with a message when you least expect it. Be still if you want to know how to listen to your spirit.

We live hectic lives. We're often on the run, and even when we sit for a moment, we whip out our cell phones or tablets to catch up on things or numb ourselves. If you genuinely want to learn more about yourself, resist the urge to do that. Relax, and offer yourself a "time out." Give your emotions and thoughts time to settle down and just do nothing. This will allow a communication pathway from your spirit to a deeper layer of yourself. The exercise in the earlier part of the chapter suggests that being still can be literally stilling your body, regulating your breathing, and allowing your mind to be quiet. It is a mental and emotional attitude that you consciously cultivate. It's not always easy, but it's important to mature and learn about that stranger in the mirror and discover what they are all about. Many of us – myself included – don't know ourselves nearly as well as we think. All of us are on an exciting journey of self-discovery and self-exploration. But we can't force it. When you allow yourself to be silent, you may feel uncomfortable emotions like anger, sadness, or confusion. As we advised earlier, don't push these feelings away. They are valuable! Difficult and painful emotions are not shameful or wrong. No one goes through life undisturbed and unscarred. Even the Buddha was upset by life before he entered his path to enlightenment. Your "negative" emotions are not a mark against you. They do not make you weak, flawed, or broken. They are what you are feeling or thinking at this moment. They may be experiences or memories coming through your mind and are valid parts of you. These feelings are ways that your spirit is asking for healing and change. The point is you can't move forward in life, and you won't hear your spirit, if you push away the pain and force yourself to be happy. Discomfort is part of the growing process. Embrace the struggle and fully validate who you are. My mother taught me that "this too shall pass." It does.

Another deeply meaningful way to reach into your mind, body, and soul is through meditation. Meditation is trendy for a reason: it works! I practice Transcendental Meditation because I have a hard time staying focused. When I meditate with a mantra, my mind stays more centered, and I move into a deeper state of peace. It isn't always a perfect session, but just taking the time to breathe and rest is worth the effort.

The truth is, most of us meditate haphazardly or in an overly controlling way by trying to force it to be "positive" or "without thoughts" in some way. That's just not going to happen. Thoughts come and go like raindrops. The point of mindful and meditative practice isn't to become some guru unbothered by life's problems. The point is to learn to let things be and allow space for your authentic feelings to come in, to focus and accept and validate them, whether they're negative, positive, or confusing. Once we acknowledge our feelings, we get to move on.

If you want your spirit to talk to you, you need to prepare your mind to receive real inspiration and learn to be less fascinated by the trivial thoughts that pop into your brain. It might sound contradictory, but if you want to get in touch with your spirit, you must first get in your body. Much of our confusion and mental struggles come from being disconnected from our physical existence. For years I tried to make progress in life mentally and emotionally. I repeated positive affirmations and positive "self-talk" until I was blue in the face. I read religious and spiritual texts, meditated deeply on their meaning, and was brought to tears by their wisdom. Guess what I didn't do? I didn't get any exercise. I didn't go for walks, and I didn't lift weights or do yoga. I didn't go out into my garden or dig in the soil and ignored mother nature's beauty. When I finally started doing those things, everything began to turn around.

There is something special about the great outdoors that nothing else can match. It can revive and energize every part of our being. Our spirit comes out of hiding and shares wisdom and healing with us. I've gone through plenty of challenging and lonely periods in my life. During those times, I didn't need my mind or intellectual ideas to tell me there was hope or a purpose to my existence; I needed fresh air, exercise, and sunshine to take me to a better frame of mind.

Pay close attention to what your spirit is telling you. If you've practiced the advice mentioned here and found it helpful, you need to do one more thing when it comes to hearing your spirit. You actually have to listen to it. Sometimes that's harder than it sounds. Your spirit may have told you very clearly that it's time to set out on a new path, leave an old relationship, study a new subject, switch careers or move to a new place and start a different life. Or your spirit may have told you to practice patience and stay in your current space and situation even though it's making you suffer. It may tell you that you have something valuable to learn and much room left to grow in your current predicament. Both of these types of scenarios can be things we simply don't want to hear. That's why it's vital to truly listen to what your soul is telling you, even if it's not your first, ego-driven, or desire-driven choice that you'd otherwise make. However, I want to add a caveat here: Never listen to what you think is your spirit if it tells you to physically or emotionally harm yourself or another person, get revenge, or give up on life. That's not your soul; it's your ego looking for a shortcut. Abiding by that will conjure up trouble.

It takes time, effort, and desire to learn how to genuinely love your life, but I can tell you that it is worth it. Get to know yourself. Learn more about your strengths and weaknesses and how they affect your decisions and interactions. When you understand who you are, you can be more in love with the life you've designed.

Empower Others

"When you think about growing and being empowered yourself,
it is what you've been able to do for other people
that leaves you the fullest."
~ Oprah Winfrey

I grew up in an unconventional household. My parents were wonderful people; they just had a unique way of managing our family life. As I mentioned, my dad's work took him away for long periods of time. My mom, tired of being a "single parent," would often jaunt off on travels with her friends or stay with my dad for a few months. Needless to say, I didn't have much supervision, and my sister and I were often left on our own. The situation left me disoriented. I loved my parents, who were highly revered in our community. Our friends, neighbors and extended family showed respect for my parents' decisions, which was perplexing. I often wondered why no one stepped in to say, "Why are those kids on their own?" I looked everywhere for validation that it wasn't typical or healthy for us to fend for ourselves.

I eventually found comfort from my high school physical education teacher, Mrs. Hadrich. I remember walking by her office one day when she asked me, "Are you okay?" I was surprised and relieved that someone finally saw that I was suffering inside. Mrs. H invited me to sit with her and talk about what was happening in my life. She wanted to hear my story because she cared about me. She listened attentively to my words and my pain. It was a relief to unburden myself to a compassionate adult. I was astonished when she shared details about her personal life with me. She explained that her childhood was turbulent, with her dad having alcoholism, and she could truly understand the anguish I was experiencing. Mrs. H helped me comprehend that my parents' behavior was not a reflection on me and that I did not need to own their decisions. She helped me see that I could succeed even if my mom and dad weren't available to support me. She heard my heart. She knew I needed validation and someone to guide me toward a brighter future.

The gratitude I have for her is immeasurable. Without her act of compassion toward me, I can only imagine where I'd be today. I was only 13 or 14 years old then, but the experience led me to understand that I was in charge of my life. It was empowering for a well-respected adult and well-regarded community member to hear me and care about my welfare. Her kindness fueled me through those tumultuous, lonely, and scary times. Because of her, I learned how cathartic it could be to open up and share my vulnerabilities with people who genuinely care about my health and well-being. These benevolent beings are hard to find. I've taken on this mission to help others learn how to share and show concern through compassionate listening because it is the rarest and most essential component of human communication.

As stated earlier, it's uncommon to find people who understand the term "compassionate listening," let alone practice the habit. It takes time to cultivate the skills necessary for productive conversation because active listening isn't just about letting others speak; it's offering emotional support and encouraging exploration of thought; it's allowing the speaker to feel understood without judgment. There are many components to its mastery. For example, when we pay attention to the person speaking to us, we let them know their opinion is valued. When we focus on their message, we can see things from their perspective and learn more about their life experiences. Typically, when we discover something about someone's history, our curiosity is piqued, and we are inclined to utter the phrase "tell me more." When someone hears that, they are prompted to share more intimate details about their life. As the conversation continues, a mutual bond of trust and respect is formed. In her book *Tell Me More*, Kelly Corrigan says, "That's how it works: someone …believes in us….and over time, we begin to believe in ourselves." Many of us don't know the rules for active listening, but we do know how much we appreciate it when someone offers the courtesy. It is a crucial component of successful communication and negotiation.

While researching for this book, I stumbled across the U.S. Department of State Diplomacy in Action site. I was fascinated to see the Chinese symbol "to listen" featured prominently on the website. In fact, the *only* thing on the site at that time was a document highlighting the foundation of successful diplomacy. It is a written treatise about the importance of listening!! Imagine that? Since it is a government-approved document, I didn't think I should tamper with it, so everything is listed verbatim here:

United States of America
Department of State Diplomacy in Action

The most common problem in communication is not listening! A Chinese symbol for "To Listen" is shown below. It is wise beyond the art. The left side of the symbol represents an ear. The right side represents the individual- you. The eyes and undivided attention are next, and finally, there is the heart.

This symbol tells us that to listen we must use both ears, watch and maintain eye contact, give undivided attention, and finally, be empathetic. In other words, we must engage in active listening! Active listening is a skill taught to teachers and police officers, counselors, ministers, rabbis, and priests. It is a skill we would all do better having learned and practiced. To begin being an active listener, we must first understand the four rules of active listening.

The Four Rules of Active Listening

1. *Seek to understand before you seek to be understood*

2. *Be non-judgmental*

3. *Give your undivided attention to the speaker*

4. *Use silence effectively*

    Let's explore the rules of active listening.

1. **Seek to understand before seeking to be understood.** *When we seek to understand rather than be understood, our modus operandi will be to listen. Often, when we enter into conversation, our goal is to be better understood. We can be better understood if first we better understand. With age, maturity, and experience comes silence. It is most often a wise person who says little or nothing at the beginning of a conversation or listening experience. We need to remember to collect information before we disseminate it. We need to know it before we say it.*

2. **Be non-judgmental.** *Empathetic listening demonstrates a high degree of emotional intelligence. There is a reason kids do not usually speak with adults about drugs, sex, and rock and roll. The kids already know what the adults have to say. Once a child knows your judgment, there is little reason to ask the question unless the intention is to argue. If we would speak to anyone about issues important to them, we need to avoid sharing our judgment until we have learned their judgment. This empathetic behavior is an indicator of emotional intelligence.*

3. **Give your undivided attention to the speaker.** *The Chinese symbol that we used to describe listening used the eyes and undivided attention. Absolutely important is dedicating your undivided*

attention to the speaker if you are to succeed as an active listener. Eye contact is less important. In most listening situations, people use eye contact to affirm listening. The speaker maintains eye contact to be sure the listener or listeners are paying attention. From their body language, the speaker can tell if he is speaking too softly or loudly, too quickly or slowly, or if the vocabulary or the language is inappropriate. Listeners can also send messages to speakers using body language. Applause is the reason many performers perform. Positive feedback is an endorphin releaser for the giver and the sender. Eye contact can be a form of positive feedback. BUT, eye contact can also be a form of aggression, of trying to show dominance, of forcing submissive behavior. All primates use eye contact to varying degrees. We should be careful how we use it when listening. If we want to provide undivided attention to a child, a better way to show your attention is to do a "walk and talk." Walk and talk is such a successful strategy that works well for active listening!

4. ***Use silence effectively.*** *The final rule for active or empathic listening is to use silence effectively. Too often, a truly revealing moment is never brought to fruition because of an untimely interruption. Some of the finest police interrogators, counselors, teachers, and parents learn more by maintaining silence than by asking questions. As an active or empathic listener, silence is a very valuable tool. DO NOT interrupt unless absolutely necessary. Silence can be painful. It is more painful for a speaker than for a listener. If someone is speaking, and we want them to continue talking, we do not interrupt. Rather, we do provide positive feedback using body language, eye contact, and nonword sounds*

like "uh, huh." Silence is indeed golden, especially when used to gather information as a listener.

Hi friends, It's me again.

The only thing to add to these wise words is this:

LISTEN & SILENT use the same letters.

We can practice many empowering communication skills to help ourselves and others. I'm sure no one is surprised to learn that we increase the speaker's self-esteem and confidence when we listen well. Our verbal and non-verbal responses help them understand that they are important to us and that we aren't judging them.

A skilled listener provides encouraging responses to help the speaker's ideas flow. A person who cares will take time to smile. It sounds so simple, but displaying a positive attitude at the start of a conversation can go a long way in putting everyone in the right mindset. A genuine smile can help the speaker feel safe and heard and that they matter.

While listening may be the best skill for effective communication, our choice of words when responding is also valuable. Open-ended statements like "tell me more," "help me understand," and "how did that make you feel?" strengthen the connection with the speaker, and help them feel that you genuinely care about them and what they are saying.

When we talk about things that matter to us, we send non-verbal signals. Some examples of wordless communication are body position, facial expression, hand movements, gestures, eye contact, attitude, tone of voice, muscle tension, and how we breathe. How we look, listen, create, react, and gesture speaks far more about feelings than words. Our responses to the speaker can encourage or discourage them. A pat on the hand or back can reassure them and help them feel confident. Stress can sometimes be helpful during conversations but can also negatively affect communication, clarity of opinion, and appropriate behaviors and actions. When under pressure, it's common to misunderstand the context of conversations, and we may send off confusing or rude non-verbal signals.

We've all felt stressed during a discussion, and we've all said and done things that we've regretted. Effective communication requires us to exercise stress management skills. It's helpful to focus on the end goal and be collaborative instead of combative. It's also a good idea to take notes, ask for clarification during conversations, and not jump to conclusions too quickly. A tip I use to avoid those subsequent regrets is emotion control. Emotion control or emotion regulation is exactly what you think it is. It's how we manage and control our emotions, or precisely, our emotional reactions. It's staying calm when handling minor problems and reacting with the proper emotional response given the situation. Challenges with emotional regulation can often cause negative issues with social skills. Learning how to have an even-keel emotional reaction to every situation allows us time to delay our response and address problems appropriately.

We all know that feelings play an important role in everything we do. Decision-making typically affects the way we feel more than the way we think. When emotions guide us, our non-verbal behavior affects how people perceive us. If you are not aware of your feelings, you cannot adequately express your needs and experiences; this results in frustration, misunderstanding, and conflict. When we control our emotions, we can better understand others and send accurate verbal and non-verbal messages. This is true for all of us. When we communicate, we want to feel heard, and that's why it's important to express ourselves effectively, but it's also just as important to listen effectively. There are some really simple rules to use for effective listening.

Rules For Effective Listening

Rule # 1. Stop talking. You can't speak and listen at the same time. These rules also apply to talking inside your head. If you are thinking intently about what you want to say, you are not listening to what is being said.

Rule # 2. Create space. Create space in your mind for the speaker and what they are saying. Create a pause between your thoughts and what you are hearing. Think of listening as a form of meditation. Quiet your mind, get all the rubbish out, and focus solely on the person talking. React and respond to what is being said instead of thinking about your response. Pay attention to how the speaker is conveying the information. Are they anxious? What is their body language? What emotion do you hear in their voice? Pay close attention to these expressions so you can respond accordingly and recognize that sometimes a reply isn't even required. Occasionally, a nod of the head or a thoughtful look are the only things people need.

Rule # 3. Hold your judgment. We often get wrapped up in what people are saying; we conjure up a passionate response we'd like to deliver, but the speaker hasn't even finished telling their story. We assume we know what will be said, so we prematurely interject our thoughts. Restraining ourselves and refraining from responding until the entire story is told allows us to respond respectfully and appropriately.

Rule # 4. Don't be a label reader. It drives me crazy, especially in our heightened political climate, that people are pigeonholed into categories. Just because someone identifies as a liberal or conservative and does something inappropriate doesn't mean all liberals or conservatives are like that. We need to cut out that type of rhetoric and look at people as the unique individuals that they are. I don't identify as a liberal, a conservative, a democrat, or a republican. I am a human being first, then an American and a person of the world. Politics isn't the only arena where labels are present. They are used to describe what geographic region we live in and our level of education. The lists go on and on. When we stop labeling people and assuming their opinions, we will have much healthier relationships and better dialogue as a nation.

Rule # 5: Open your mind. Being open-minded is at the top of the list when it comes to traits and habits you need to acquire to be a happy person. An open mind allows us to stretch our thoughts, knowledge, and ideas beyond our self-constructed boundaries, making us more adaptable to unique environments. Showing acceptance of different cultures, genders, races, ethnicities, and ages helps us learn more about the world around us. We can build a more harmonious relationship with whoever we meet by simply recognizing and respecting others' beliefs and practices. Being open-minded can help us put our differences aside and cooperate to progress as individuals and as a society. If we want to inspire others, we need to be open to and learn from a variety of people. This strength helps us form meaningful and lasting relationships.

Compassionate listening is an empowering tool. Being interested in others and giving them space to be who they are and feel what they feel validates their existence and their right to pursue their goals and dreams. If we try, every one of us can mentor people to their highest ideal.

Act on Opportunity

"Your big opportunity may be right where you are now."
~ Napoleon Hill

Academics and extracurricular pursuits interested me as a kid, but I couldn't devote much time to them. My parents were often out of the picture, so I bounced between the homes of extended family and friends. Never wanting to be a burden or an added expense to them, I worked to help earn my keep. I was a dish-washer, waitress, cleaning lady, and nanny. At one point, I worked as a mom's helper to a hairdresser. She was one of those hovering moms, so I mostly spent time in her makeshift salon on her porch. I swept up hair, washed and folded towels and helped remove curlers from people's hair. It wasn't long until I picked up a side gig cutting hair.

I had no idea what I was doing, but I eventually gave haircuts to anyone who asked. It was fun, so I expanded my skills and learned how to offer other services. I enjoyed working hard and making money, but I really wanted a good education and an opportunity to attend college. The adults in my life at that time were kind and insightful. Many saw my potential and recognized that I needed extra support and guidance. Since it appeared I had a natural knack for hairdressing, and because it was more affordable than college, my high school principal, Mr. Perrine, advised me to go to a trade school. As soon as I heard the idea, I knew it was the best thing to do. So, I set a goal to earn enough money as a hairdresser to pay for my college education. Well, sometimes things don't work out as planned. I ended up at cosmetology school and went on to have a very successful and lucrative career. I eventually went to college, but because my career took off like a rocket, I didn't finish. While I regret not completing that dream, my life turned out well. Countless lucky breaks have come my way; I am beyond grateful for the experiences that allowed me to meet many intelligent and influential mentors. The people who believed in me showed me how to identify and grab hold of "once in a lifetime" opportunities. I am thankful that my intuition and common sense encouraged me to listen to them.

When I started life on my own, I got a job working for a delightful couple who had a decadent lifestyle. They lived in south Florida in a gorgeous mansion on the water. They often entertained friends and hosted glorious parties. They hired me to help at these fancy shindigs. It was lots of fun, and the compensation was outstanding. I loved the work, and I loved them. And, as luck would have it, they loved me too.

After working for them for a few months, they extended an invitation for me to move into their palatial palace with them. This was a welcomed and very luxurious change of pace because, at the time, I was living out of my suitcase and staying with various friends. In my new home, I had private quarters and dedicated parking, where I put the brand-new car they bought for me. These amazing people treated me like their child. They never tired of spoiling me. They took me shopping for new clothes and introduced me to a new and exciting way of life. They brought me to elaborate dinner parties and charity balls. I flew on their private jet, sailed on their yacht, and met fascinating and powerful people. It was, without a doubt, the most pivotal experience of my life.

They, too, came from humble beginnings, so they understood the immense learning curve I was experiencing and helped me avoid missteps. They also steered me toward new opportunities —things I couldn't even dream of because I had little knowledge of that way of life. At first, it was intimidating to be in that environment, but I kept my eyes and ears wide open. I listened and quickly learned how to navigate the unfamiliar terrain, eventually gaining the ability to firmly stand on my own two feet and move forward in life in a direction I never knew existed. I don't know what my life would look like had I not met those kind-hearted, generous friends. They changed the trajectory of my existence and made a permanent difference in my life. They cared about me and my future and showed me what is possible if you dream big and work hard.

I eventually took positions with well-known companies and worked my way up the leadership chain. I am married to the man of my dreams, and we have two wonderful children. We've lived all over the country and have traveled the world. I am in awe of the life I've experienced thus far. The tough times I went through helped me find inner resolve, and they taught me how to focus and benefit from opportunities presented to me. I cannot tell you how many people opened doors for me and gave me rich and meaningful experiences. I am grateful that I am now in a position to do the same for others. The paying-it-forward formula is a ripple effect of kindness that everyone can appreciate. Every one of us has the ability to make a difference in the lives of others.

One of my favorite motivational speakers, Zig Ziglar, said, "You can have everything you want in life if you help other people get what they want." It's true. Life is best lived when we're in service to others. When we lend a hand to our family, co-workers, friends, and strangers, we experience joy and satisfaction that can't be achieved by any other means. Extending ourselves to others helps us gain opportunities, happiness, and excitement.

But if you think opportunities and rewards will just fall into your lap, you are in for a big surprise. Believe it or not, lucky breaks materialize because we manifest and attract them. Our daily habits and routines help us get recognized by the outside world. When word gets out that you are open-minded and self-assured, opportunities can and will come your way. People adore optimism and confidence. Viewing the world as a place for enjoyment sends off positive signals that you're open to opportunities and ready to receive them. As I mentioned, good things don't just happen. You have to work for them. You must keep honing your skills, sharing your accomplishments, and sending out good vibes.

New opportunities can't get to you if they don't know where to find you, so get out there and let people know you are open to new experiences. The best way to do that is through networking. In its purest form, networking is people enjoying other people, communicating passions, and connecting with others who share those passions. It's listening, figuring out what others need, and connecting them with people you think can help without any designs for personal gain. The most successful networkers build genuine relationships and give more than they receive. When you have no ulterior motive, you can build relationships and a reputation for being generous rather than self-serving. Since every person has value, it's essential that you know what yours is. Before you start networking, get clear on what talents, strengths, skill sets, and connections you can offer and map out how you may be able to help other people, either now or in the future. While you may be tempted to network to land a job, that's a mistake.

Instead, make it your goal to be open, friendly, and honest and forge connections between people who may be able to help each other. Generosity is an attractive quality, and it's something special that people will remember about you. So, make it your mission to discover the value in each person you talk to. Ask questions and listen with interest. Please don't make the mistake of discounting people due to their titles. Someone you meet may "just" be a clerk, but they may have valuable connections or knowledge you'd never learn about if you'd dismissed them. Once you begin to listen to people and learn what they can bring to the table, you'll start realizing how one person may be able to help another.

Make it a point to connect people you feel have something of genuine value to each other. When you go out of your way to make those potentially promising connections, you do your part to help others and yourself succeed. If you believe that the true value of networking lies in helping others and you do your part, you'll soon discover magic happening all around you.

And remember, if you stay where it's always cozy, you've got no chance to grow. Step outside your comfort zone, meet new people, and land in new situations. The more information you put out there about your areas of expertise, the more people will recognize your name and think of you as an authority. When you give back to others in the form of knowledge, you are also giving back to yourself and developing a reputation as a trusted professional.

By establishing yourself as someone who knows what they're about, your chances of getting opportunities and offers will increase exponentially. The more developed, well-rounded, and ambitious you are, the more opportunities you can nab. So, to make sure you're not stagnant or slowing down in your self-development, check in with your progress every month and see where you can bump up the energy. Being systematic in your actions is important because they will increase your chances in the long term to attract plenty of new options.

Finally, the most important thing I've done to increase my opportunities is to have a good mentor. I've had so many and have learned a great deal from each of them. These goodhearted souls have guided me and given me uncomfortable feedback when needed. But they have also vouched for my hard-working nature and intelligence. My mentors have introduced me to influential people who have helped me meet personal and professional goals. Many untapped opportunities are waiting for you, too. So put yourself out there and take a leap of faith.

Taking risks in relationships allows us to have less fear about trying something new. Science backs this up. Multiple studies have been done about the effects of altruism, which is the selfless concern for the well-being of others. According to one report from the University of Wisconsin-Madison, researchers found that individuals polled in their mid-30s who rated helping others as necessary stated they were happier with their lives when surveyed 30 years later. Scientists say the sensation is known as "helpers high." It is produced when your brain releases feel-good chemicals called endorphins. When you do something kind for someone, your brain's pleasure centers light up and send you a boost of healthy mental energy.

A study published in *Psychological Science* found that thinking about times you've helped others will make you want to help others again. The research found that reflecting on your past good deeds makes you feel selfless and wanting to help more people, compared with reflecting on the times others have helped you. In other words, thinking about what you've given others - and not only what you've received — will motivate you to do good again and again. You might be asking yourself where to start. Sometimes offering help to others can be as simple as smiling at them or striking up a random conversation with someone. Society has become so drenched in technology buzz that real face-to-face interaction and authentic relationships are growing scarce. Next time you throw out the standard, "Hi, how are you?" make an effort to listen to the reply and invest time developing a respectful rapport. Being friendly to others is a great way to brighten someone's day. Whether at the store, at work, or simply walking along the street, a nice gesture like a smile could go a long way to make someone feel happy.

Suppose you want to take on something a little meatier. Volunteer! Volunteering is a fantastic experience that gets us out of our regular routines and exposes us to many interesting people. Many not-for-profit agencies can use your time, talent, and treasure. Do a simple Google search, find out which organizations pique your interest, and give them a call.

You can make an effort to assist in fundamental ways. Donating to a food pantry is a fantastic way to spend your time and money, especially in this economic climate. Care packages are affordable, easy to assemble, and can be distributed in various ways. You can put together a pal pack for work colleagues that includes headache meds, a lint roller, and a Tide pen. Another idea is a snack pack for people in need. It can consist of non-perishable food items, a water bottle, and/or a gift certificate to a restaurant. Keep a supply in your car and give them to people who need a little cheering up. A kind gesture goes a long way.

Volunteering at local events and picking up trash in your city are other great ways to give back to your community. There are tons of organizations looking for people to sponsor in-need children in the US and countries around the world. Signing up is easy and affordable. It is a small price to make a big difference in a child's life. You also might consider teaching a skill to someone who wants to learn something specific that interests both of you. It might be teaching someone how to drive or helping a student with homework. Whatever it is, your lessons will have a massive impact on their lives.

If you're a typical American, you have a lot of stuff, so when it comes time to get rid of things, donate them. There are many ways to accomplish this. You can do it on online platforms or local charities in your community. And if you see someone struggling, stop what you're doing and help them. It's easy to think that our priorities are the ones that matter the most, and you'd be correct if the priority is to do good – but often, it's not that. So how about if you see someone grappling with something — maybe carrying something heavy, fixing a flat tire, picking up items they've dropped, etc., stop what you're doing and lend them a hand. Think about it; if you were in their shoes, wouldn't you want a little assistance, too? Look around. There are multiple ways to help and offer support.

If you're not ready to roll solo, consider teaming up with someone. It can make the work less intimidating and help you contribute twice as much. If you don't already know this, having a partner is the best kind of motivation out there. So why not give it a go? It will significantly impact their lives, and together, you'll be on your way to a healthier life.

It's sad but true; we live in a self-centered society. Many of us participate in activities that help make us most successful, leading us to do self-serving things. It's important to consider what's in the best interest of all and turn our self-centered gaze outward. Taking time to put others' needs before yours empowers everyone and leads to opportunities you've never dreamed of.

Do Good

"Carve your name on hearts, not tombstones. A legacy is etched into the minds of others and the stories they share about you."
~ Sharon Addler

Stephen R. Covey's book, *The 7 Habits of Highly Effective People,* is basically a recipe book for a healthy life. I turn to it often to help me stay grounded and focused on doing the right things for myself, my loved ones, and my community. I'm reminded that the way I see the world is based on my perceptions and that, if I want to change a situation, I need to change the way I think about it because my thoughts are just thoughts, and they shift when I put on new "perspectacles." Another big takeaway from Covey's book is starting with the end in mind. Covey urges us to imagine being at our own funeral. During the ceremony, four people are going to speak about you: a close family member, a dear friend, a work colleague, and someone from your community. Think deeply.

What would you like these people to say about you and how you lived your life? What values, contributions, and achievements do you want them to remember? What difference would you like to have made in their lives? Dedicate some time to considering the imaginary funeral speeches from your loved ones. Repeat the practice from time to time to keep a fresh and positive mindset. If you carefully contemplate what you want to be said of you, you can mold the life you want and devote time to the people and things that really matter to you. Doing so will bring you untold joy and far fewer regrets. Well-adjusted, successful people cultivate a servant's heart. A servant's heart means to have a mindset or a desire to selflessly and compassionately serve others, regardless of your feelings towards them. A passage from the Bible explains it far better than I can.

Philippians 2:3–5 *³ When you do things, do not let selfishness or pride be your guide. Instead, be humble and give more honor to others than to yourselves. ⁴ Do not be interested only in your own life but be interested in the lives of others.*

Doing good means acting in principled and honorable ways toward others and unconditionally lending your time, money, and effort for the benefit of all. Much like a soldier, a servant must always be standing by for duty. They must be willing for schedules to be interrupted to do what's required, even if it's inconvenient. Opportunities to serve can often be missed when we lack sensitivity and spontaneity. We don't get to wait for the right time to make a difference. We get to seize opportunities when they arise. There's never room for procrastinating or excuses. If your heart is in the right space, you always have the right tools to do good, so don't let the fear of "not being good enough" stop you. A servant's heart is revealed by performing the most minor tasks and acting in thoughtful ways that others don't. Servant leaders are trustworthy and dependable. Their integrity cannot be moved. They follow through on promises and can be counted on by others to always do the right thing. These humble helpers keep their humility in check, maintain a low profile, and never serve for the approval or applause of others. They simply live to serve. This is where the rubber meets the road. Doing things for the sake of doing good is where it's at. Throughout this book, we have examined what it means to serve others by listening with compassion and empathy, and as you've recognized, these themes often run together. Loving one's life equates to empowering others, acting on opportunity, and doing good. Now it's time to take it to the next level and look at how you can leave a meaningful legacy using your servant's heart.

Planning charity events is one of the jobs I have loved the most over the years. It is a fantastic feeling when people come together for a unified purpose to contribute good. The professional relationship that touched me the most was the one I shared with the founders of the Up With Down Syndrome Foundation. I spent many years volunteering for this organization in Miami and was filled with hope every day that I was there. Dr. Michael and Camille Geraldi founded the organization. They had a calling to care for children with special needs. Together, the two have adopted or become the guardians of eighty-eight children with various physical and mental conditions, including Down's Syndrome, spina bifida, cardiac problems, and many other diagnoses.

The Geraldis have two biological children, and, as a family, they have devoted themselves to their mission of giving special needs babies a joy-filled life. They built a compound with three homes where their children —along with their aides and medical teams, could grow up in an environment where their unique requirements could be met in a loving and caring manner. Through the years, the Geraldis have focused on helping their children learn to do what they can – rather than what they can't, and as a result, they have exceeded the expectations of family, friends, doctors, and the birth parents of the children they care for.

All that was put in jeopardy when a devastating hurricane ravaged their homes. The property was torn to shreds, and the houses sustained damage to the roofs and windows. They needed help, and they needed it fast. I had connections to a group of volunteers who eagerly jumped in line to assist the Geraldis. We all pitched in, and within a few weeks, the houses were habitable, and the grounds were pristine again.

In the meantime, I pulled together a fundraiser that brought in thousands of dollars to get the foundation back on track. Being in service to that family was very rewarding. Their selfless acts of caring for special needs children sparked something in me - and all the volunteers. We learned that doing things out of desire instead of obligation or duty brings untold satisfaction and contentment. It's been decades, but that experience kickstarted my volunteering journey. Since then, I have been involved with or spearheaded hundreds of initiatives to bring comfort, joy, and peace to society. Every effort has brought me fulfillment and immeasurable delight. There are myriad ways to contribute good to your community, but I believe volunteering from your heart makes the most significant impact because it's selfless. It is a theme that runs through this book —and in my life. I know firsthand that being in service to others provides a healthy boost of self-confidence, self-esteem, and life satisfaction. Doing good for the sake of doing good gives us a natural sense of accomplishment. Your role as a volunteer can also give you a sense of pride and identity.

For many years, my job title was Director of Special Events. I worked for Sony Records, CNN, the International Olympic Committee, and other well-known agencies. The experiences were nothing short of incredible. But success isn't just about making money and meeting fancy people; it includes making a difference in people's lives. Yes, I made money and met famous and fascinating people, but none of that compares to my work as a volunteer. Volunteering helps us develop a support system of like-minded individuals. Together you can make a remarkable impact on society. There are countless ways to contribute good. As I mentioned, every community has at least one charitable organization, so find a cause you're passionate about and organize on its behalf. You can collect money to support their mission or do something on a smaller scale. You don't have to orchestrate grand gestures to make a difference. Offering help to an elderly neighbor or parent of a newborn can go a long way too. There are always folks in your neighborhood who could use a hand. You can go grocery shopping, carry their trash to the curb, rake their leaves, or shovel snow for them.

The gesture doesn't really matter as long as you're showing you care. We've all heard the benefits of performing random acts of kindness, but I believe deliberate acts of kindness are equally, if not more, impactful. When we make appointments to help others, we are more invested in the outcome. You might offer to teach English as a Second Language (ESL) or tutor a struggling student. Being a mentor to someone who can benefit from your skills, knowledge, and experience is a beautiful way to spend your time. There are plenty of ordinary and obvious ways to add value to your community. For example, shop locally. Doing so celebrates small businesses and helps communities flourish.

Spending money at hometown retailers and restaurants props up the local economy and keeps your money moving in a cycle of reinvestment. Avoid the convenience trap of Amazon and other online retailers, and make an effort to support local retailers; doing so helps everyone in your community thrive. Attending council, committee, and board meetings is another excellent way to contribute to your community. Knowing your neighborhood's issues and challenges will prompt you to take action and find ways to solve problems. Participating in local government helps you develop a sense of ownership and belonging. Your involvement will offer untold good to your community.

If attending meetings isn't your thing, try gardening. Most municipalities dedicate an area of town where residents gather to plant produce and flowers. These gardens beautify the community and often provide fresh vegetables to residents and food pantries. Whether you have a green thumb or are just beginning a relationship with the land, there's always lots of fun to be had. You won't just be growing a garden, but friendships and community along the way. Another area that always requires time, attention, and compassion is animal shelters. Animal shelters play a vital role in our communities because they continuously reunite pets with foster families and permanent homes. Working with pets and other animals is highly gratifying. Our family has fostered eleven puppies and given homes to dozens of pets through the years, including our four adopted dogs.

The experience was fun and rewarding, and it introduced us to people we may not have otherwise met. Studies show that caring for animals can significantly improve your mood and can help reduce stress and anxiety. I can attest to that first-hand. My husband and I went through a low period after our son left for college. He was the youngest child, so we became empty-nesters when he flew the coop. We fostered a few puppies, and suddenly we had a purpose in our lives again.

If pets aren't your thing, consider giving your time to people who live in assisted living facilities or nursing homes. Many live far from their families and suffer from hopelessness and helplessness. They need attention and validation, just like the rest of us. My favorite grandmother lived in a nursing home, and I visited her often. She loved it when I would paint her fingernails, wash her feet and brush her hair.

She enjoyed it so much that she decided I should make my services available to the other residents. I was happy to do it because I could see how much they enjoyed and appreciated the pampering. Spending my time indulging my grandma and her friends was an honor and an incredibly satisfying way to use my time. The experience was likely far more gratifying for me than it was for them, that I am sure of. So don't hold back. Find something you are passionate about and make an effort to positively impact even one person's life. I promise you; you won't regret it.

CHAPTER FOUR

It's Up To You

"Too often, we underestimate the power of a touch, smile, a kind word, a listening ear, an honest compliment, or the smallest act of caring, all of which have the potential to turn a life around."
~ Leo Buscaglia

We rarely find books to read and reread – frequently. *The Four Agreements* is that kind of book for me. When I read it the first time, I learned how to love myself more, not take things personally, and start healing my relationships. Repeatedly rereading the book unlocks more insight into why I am the way I am. I found that my lack of self-love created needless suffering in my everyday life. I also understood the source of my self-limiting beliefs, which helped me recognize how I rob myself of joy. This book has left a lasting impression on me, and I trust this simple read will do the same for you. It's a practical guide to help you feel self-assured and confident by committing to four easy agreements. They are contracts you make with yourself to help you stop punishing yourself for not being what you believe you should be.

The Four Agreements are:

1. **Be impeccable with your word.** Words are powerful. They can be encouraging or discouraging. It's important to think carefully before using them on yourself and others and to develop a habit of only saying what you mean and meaning what you say. Doing so will save you untold pain and suffering. If you're unsure how to respond to a situation, it's best to say nothing.

2. **Don't take anything personally.** If you take things personally, you're likely in a self-absorbed mindset and believe everything is about "you," which is a selfish way to operate. When people share their opinions, it is a window into their world. Their words and actions are products of their reality and have nothing to do with you. Staying mindful of this will help you defuse their statements' power and lessen their impact on you. There's a tremendous amount of freedom that comes when you don't absorb the opinion of others.

3. **Don't make assumptions.** Most assumptions aren't based on reality anyway, but we often give them validation as if they are. This results in misunderstandings and suffering. You can avoid all this if you keep an old saying in mind, "When you assume, you make an ASS out of U and Me." It's best to ask questions to clarify, and if you make an assumption, be sure it's generous. Stay mindful and cautious of your natural tendency to assume things about yourself, others, and the world around you. Instead, look and listen without labels or judgment.

4. **Always do your best.** I was taught that what's worth doing is worth doing well. Putting your best effort into whatever you attempt is a way of showing respect for yourself. Your best will change from time to time depending on how you're feeling physically, mentally, and emotionally. Still, as you become more mindful of the principles delivered in this book, your best will get better day by day; just keep practicing! Doing so will help you better understand yourself and allow you to experience true happiness and love.

Applying these contracts to your daily life will give you a deeper appreciation and understanding of yourself and the people in your life. With this awareness will come an unconditional acceptance of whatever comes your way. You will learn to speak more succinctly and avoid passive/aggressive discussions. You'll understand that sharing your honest thoughts and intentions in a loving way is an efficient way to navigate through conversations – and life. Recognizing that others' behaviors reflect how they feel inside will give you the desire to offer them grace, and you'll start to avoid making guesses about circumstances you can't control. Eventually, you will develop the habit of giving your best effort in every situation. But again, all this takes practice, and no one can do any of this perfectly.

Using the tenants in *The Four Agreements* taught me the value of letting things go and forgiving myself and others. I have a motto now that I've lived by for more than a decade, and it is: forgiveness is the only gift I give because it's the only gift I want. It's true. A few years back, I recognized that I had let anger and resentment build up in me for far too long. It was impacting my relationships and my daily life in brutal ways. My mental, physical and emotional health was suffering. I cried all the time; if I wasn't crying, I'd either yell or hide. It was hell for everyone. I tried talking to friends about it, but they wanted to give me their unsolicited advice, so I decided to get professional help. I found an excellent therapist, and much to my surprise, she didn't offer me any advice. All she did was listen to me. All that talking helped me get to the root of my issues, and I discovered how mad I was at myself for past transgressions. I offered heaping amounts of grace to myself and felt healed from all the pain I had been suffering. I cannot express the level of peace and freedom I know now. Forgiveness truly is the greatest triumph of life.

I continue to work hard to forgive myself quickly and not hold grudges against those who have trespassed against me. I do this because it helps me live a more balanced and productive life. Sure, plenty of people have intentionally tried to hurt me. But their actions speak far louder about what's happening inside them than it does about their grievances against me. Extending these poor souls grace, even for a moment, has lifted a weight from my shoulders that I had long forgotten I carried. Forgiveness unlocks the space, energy, and strength needed to reshape your reality by eliminating old, damaging thoughts and preventing new, unwanted ones from taking root. Extending heartfelt forgiveness to yourself and others is the key to inner freedom.

There is no denying that we survive and thrive on the kindness of others. Civilization is the product of social organization and social arrangements, so I would be remiss if I didn't mention the importance of friendships. The older I get, the more I recognize how grateful I am to have many treasured friends. Developing and maintaining healthy relationships isn't easy, though. It involves give-and-take. Sometimes, we give support; other times, we're on the receiving end. My husband taught me to treat our relationship like an emotional bank account. Every act of kindness and every expression of gratitude is deposited into the account, while criticism and negativity draw down the account.

I also maintain this philosophy in my friendships, and it works out well. All my friends are lovely people who generously give their time to me. If I feel I've neglected someone in my friend network, I usually send them a quick text to tell them I'm thinking of them and that I love them. Yes, I frequently say to my friends that I love them and why. I do this because it's true and because I want them to know how much I value them. Most of us interact with a lot of people in a day. Because you're reading this book, I'm going to assume that you, like me, are a kind, inviting, and supportive person. Warm and thoughtful individuals like us can create the foundation for friendships when interacting with others. But until you and another person both invest in establishing a relationship, you are just acquaintances.

Friendships begin with reciprocity, but to flourish, they require loyalty, empathetic concern, honesty, thoughtfulness, connection, and trust. If you want to widen your circle of friends, you might need to take the initial risk and ante up an authentic connection. Friendship is much more than a simple transactional exchange. The bonds that are built over the sharing of time, resources, and presence are the bonds that deepen over time. Being brave and sharing our worst and hardest struggles is the glue that keeps us all connected. I wish more people understood that. Naturally, not all friendships are meant to last forever. People change; we grow up, and we grow apart, and if we're honest, we can realize that every relationship teaches us something valuable about ourselves and others. The duration of a friendship doesn't define its worth. Sometimes, things just aren't meant to be. If someone strays away to do their own thing, we need to move on. We can't beat ourselves up or wonder where we went wrong; chances are, it had nothing to do with us anyway. Still, losing a friend is complicated and is something most people dread. Our social supports are essential and directly relate to our mental and emotional well-being. Friends support and remind us of our value — even when things get tricky.

True friends stand by us when we're adjusting to a new change and keep us grounded in reality. The bond I share with my friends gives meaning to my life. My closest confidants have stood firmly by my side through highs and lows, celebrations and sadnesses. The appreciation I have for my precious friends knows no bounds. I consider it an honor to invest time and energy to keep our relationships strong because true, meaningful friendships are rare. The author/professor, Brené Brown, specializes in social connection. She says, "A deep sense of love and belonging is an irresistible need of all people. We are biologically, cognitively, physically, and spiritually wired to love, to be loved, and to belong. When those needs are not met, we don't function as we were meant to. We break. We fall apart. We numb. We ache. We hurt others. We get sick." Like it or not, we are social creatures. Money, power, fame, beauty, and eternal youth are at the top of the list for some people, but the root of those desires is a need to belong, be accepted, connect with others, and be loved. We pride ourselves on our independence and not depending on others, but, as psychologists have repeatedly stressed, social connection is a fundamental need. You know the moment when you meet someone new, and the two of you just "click"? Or the feeling that your significant other can read your mind? It's called 'shared reality,' and it's fantastic. A way to encourage that type of synergy is to engage in deeper and more meaningful conversations. We tend to overestimate how awkward the exchanges will be and underestimate how much we will enjoy them and how connected they will make us feel to the other person, but I promise you, it's worth the effort. Psychologists agree. In a series of experiments, people were put into pairs and told to chat about shallow topics, such as what they had recently seen on tv. Other groups discussed deeper issues, such as the last time they had cried in front of someone.

Interestingly the results showed that talking about something deeper and more personal fostered a stronger connection. The studies also found that participants consistently mispredicted the benefits of deep conversations. They thought deep discussions would be more awkward than they were and not nearly as enjoyable and meaningful as they ended up being. Most of us tend to underestimate how interested the other person is in learning about us. Because of this, we avoid divulging personal information and sometimes evade conversations altogether. Some of us are unwilling to reach out to others because we fear rejection. We often take a safer approach and wait for others to befriend us. But if we want friends, we've got to get beyond this and take the initiative to create and develop these relationships. It can be daunting at first, but it is worth the trouble. Find a club or group where people with interests like yours meet regularly. Attend workshops, sign up for a community education class, or attend a local college, senior center, or gym class. Consider volunteering for a charity. You will spread kindness and goodwill and meet compassionate people with a cause.

You may be surprised by how fast you connect with like-minded people, and when you first meet them, try to avoid that small talk. Pleasant, superficial discussions can hamper opportunities for new friendships. The reality is most people *are* interested in deep conversations because they are more enjoyable than shallow chats. Keep these findings in mind the next time you are conversing at a social event or chatting with a friend or family member on the phone or in person. You might find yourself sharing something personal and experiencing that wonderful feeling of really "clicking." Once the ice is broken, connecting and developing more meaningful relationships will be easier. Remember, human beings are hard-wired for social connection, and it has been proven that every aspect of health and well-being improves when individuals and communities are connected.

It's a balancing act.

We've covered lots of topics in this book and examined plenty of ways to do better —for ourselves, others, and our communities. We discussed marriage, children, friendships, and volunteering, but none of these associations can be completely fulfilling if we don't have balance in our lives. I've found that focusing on gratitude is the fastest way to get on solid ground. I use an effortless technique to help me remember all the things I can be grateful for. I encourage you to practice this exercise, too. Take three minutes, close your eyes, and find something to be thankful for. It doesn't have to be anything grandiose. Showing gratitude for the morning sun or the shoes on your feet is enough to get you started. As you soak into the moment, your mind will take you to a plethora of things that can bring you to awe. All of us have countless riches. When we dedicate time and attention to them, every part of our life becomes more fulfilling.

Conversely, everything can fall apart when we lose sight of our blessings. I know this first-hand because I recently experienced a real-life episode of burnout. I was in a long-term state of mental and physical exhaustion that zapped the joy out of my career, friendships, and family interactions. The continuous exposure to stressful situations —working long hours and witnessing upsetting issues related to my job in the food insecurity space, overwhelmed me. It was honestly one of the most challenging periods of my life. Because I was born with a servant's heart, I took on the responsibility of ensuring everyone in my life was cared for during the pandemic. That meant caring for my family, neighbors, and the community. I worked seven days a week for ninety-nine weeks. I coordinated multiple multi-layered projects and did the lion's share of the work because, due to the pandemic, there were very few people to whom I could delegate responsibilities. In the middle of this, my husband and I invested in a restaurant, and I also helped organize my friend's political campaign for the town council. To top it off, I was involved in a car accident that caused severe pain in my back. This continual exposure to high levels of stress completely drained me. I frequently lost my cool with friends, co-workers, and family members, and to cope with the shame and embarrassment, I drank and ate way too much. I tried to exercise, but whenever I had time for myself, I would rest instead. I gained a tremendous amount of weight and had health concerns. My heart was constantly beating out of my chest, and I developed brain fog that frequently made me lose my train of thought mid-sentence. I cried and complained every single day for months. I was awarded multiple prestigious local, state, and national recognitions, but none made me proud of my work. Toward the end of this hellish experience, I just worked to get the job done. None of it really mattered to me. I was in a perpetual state of resentment, and it did me in.

Finally, with the help of my husband, a few loyal friends, and my excellent therapist, I left my job. I took two months off and did nothing but sleep, walk my dog, and spend time with my husband and my support network. I recognize the things that did me in are mostly irrelevant in the scheme of things, and I do not in any way want to minimize the stress levels of our medical workers and frontline workers who gave everything during the pandemic. I am in awe of them and their sacrifices. My motive in sharing the details of my life is to point out that burnout is real and it can happen to anyone. It took a toll on me and my relationships. I've vowed never again to let myself into that situation –global crisis or not.

I work hard every day now to show gratitude. That is the primary thing that helps me reach and maintain a healthy balance. Balanced living means assessing your life: relationships, work, fitness and health, and emotional well-being, and taking the time to address each issue causing you unrest. Caring for yourself and indulging in creative outlets is critically important in order to be a well-adjusted person. It takes a lot of effort, but the benefits cannot be denied. Self-care is well known for reducing stress and can make you happier and more optimistic about the future. It's easy to get bogged down with other responsibilities, so we must try as hard as we can to recharge our bodies physically and mentally daily. Carving out "me time" can do a lot to bring peace to our lives. I learned personally that self-care and self-compassion are foundational to our ability to serve the world. Suppose our goal is to bring compassion to others—whether those closest to us or those suffering around our nation and the globe—we must embrace our ability to be kind to ourselves. And yet, that seems to be something many of us have a hard time doing. So do your best to schedule time each week to allow yourself to de-stress and spend a few minutes on relaxation each day. If necessary, get up a few minutes early in the morning to savor a cup of coffee and some devotional time before everyone else wakes up. Do your best to make daily activities more fun — try a new ethnic recipe for dinner, take a long soak in the tub instead of a quick shower, listen to new music, or learn a new language while you commute to work. Devote time each week to a hobby you love or learn a new one you've always wanted to try; art classes, in particular, can be stimulating and rewarding. Instead of just sitting at your desk and gobbling down lunch while you keep working, spend your lunch hour doing things you enjoy, like going for a walk, taking an exercise break, or reading a book. But be reasonable. People have a limit on resources like time, money, and energy. It is understandable to want to accomplish so many things; however, it is important to consider how much time is in a day. Know that you are *one* person, erase the idea of perfection and problem-solving for others, and know it's okay not to get everything done. Remind yourself that you are doing your best.

Most importantly, don't forget to laugh. It's great for your health and can help alleviate stress, fight infections, boost brain health, lower blood pressure, and improve mood. Self-compassion provides emotional strength and resilience, allowing us to admit our shortcomings, motivate ourselves with kindness, forgive ourselves when needed, relate wholeheartedly to others, and be more authentically ourselves. Let the people in your life who build you up and support you add value to your life and inspire you to be a better version of yourself. Try to avoid people who add or create more stress for you because stress affects us physically too; so, within reason, consider phasing out those who might be causing you anxiety or imbalance. Know that it's ok to take control and say no. Often we say yes to others because there might be a little pressure to please people immediately. It is essential to consider your current list of responsibilities. Take time to think about what you can reasonably complete and try to alleviate adding extra stress by learning how to say no. The other thing that is critically important to a balanced life is making time for rest. Resting doesn't always mean sleeping, but scheduling time to relax can benefit you greatly. Intentionally do things that give you comfort, peace, health, and happiness, and make a deliberate effort to prioritize your needs. Remember, there is more to life than the stressors that create imbalance and unhappiness. Start taking steps toward a more balanced life by learning to take control, set boundaries, and focus on today.

CHAPTER FIVE

Communication in Action

*"Communication is the solvent of all problems
and is the foundation for personal development."*
~ Peter Shepherd

I n our communication-oversaturated world, deciding whether to text, call, write, email, or message can be difficult. Suppose we didn't use any of those forms to communicate and instead relied on a more profound exchange using our hearts. The importance of this kind of heart communication cannot be understated; this book aims to help people do just that. There are many approaches. For example, eye contact, facial expressions, and physical touch are ways to connect and share emotions. But the most profound is through the spoken word. Our speech and tone of voice reveal what we think and feel about everything and everyone. I thought it would be fun to look at the evolution of communication and the different styles of expressing ourselves.

Before language developed, we strived to articulate our experiences and ideas. Linguistics research shows that mothers and caregivers have always used soothing pitches when interacting with babies and small children. The theory is that early humans made sounds to imitate things around them, like animal calls, nature, and the scraping tone of tools, which evolved into the following known form of communication: cave paintings. Fast forward to hieroglyphic writing and then the alphabet that the Phoenicians devised in 1500 BC. The Phoenician alphabet connected spoken sounds to written sounds. This created a universal way of communicating. Other written languages were derived from the Phoenician alphabet, which had 22 letters. These letters provided the basis for the Hebrew, Arabic, Greek, and eventually the Latin alphabet, which produced the modern alphabet.

The letters were strung together to create words, and words were pulled together to form sentences. Then, everything changed when emotion became part of our deeper discussions. In 1872, Charles Darwin published *The Expression of the Emotions in Man and Animal.* He argued that all humans, and even other animals, show emotion through remarkably similar behaviors. He proposed that, like other traits, emotions evolved and were adapted over time. Primal feelings, such as fear, are associated with ancient parts of the brain. Social emotions, such as guilt and pride, evolved. The notion is that the more recently developed part of the brain moderates an older part of the brain. Darwin also researched and found that our most cherished human qualities are morality and intellect. A person's morality, or lack thereof, can color how other qualities, such as friendliness and intelligence, are seen. Morality isn't something we need to calculate; it is something we feel. It is part of our very nature and exists because it benefits both us and others. According to research, it's more important to be moral than to be likable or intelligent. But it's tough to express ourselves effectively with modern-day communications. It's almost like we are back in the days of hieroglyphic writing with a mixture of the early alphabet. We now communicate with memes, emojis, and short, simple words and phrases. It isn't always easy to decipher the meaning of our exchanges or detect emotions. We need to work harder to interpret the definitions behind these writings. As such, we should be more diligent about conveying our morality and intelligence in our online and texting communications and in person-to-person exchanges. Now more than ever, we need to express empathy and compassion toward ourselves and others, which isn't easy to convey in the digital landscape.

Post-Pandemic Communication

A lot has happened in the world since I started writing this book. We experienced unimaginable upheaval as we navigated a global pandemic. That experience profoundly changed the way we communicate. I remember going for walks in the early days of the crisis and seeing our neighbors. We'd quickly turn away from one another and continue walking with our eyes focused on the ground. None of us knew if it was safe to look at each other. Not so much because we feared getting sick; I think most of us dreaded falling apart if we made eye contact. The stress was overwhelming. Eventually, when we braved the conditions and went in public, many of us wore masks. That forced us to use eye contact, hand gestures, and other non-verbal cues to communicate. In some ways, that was more meaningful than communicating with our words. We paid closer attention to the people speaking with us and worked harder to show empathy and morality by looking at each other. When we could finally interact in public, we found substitutes for handshakes and used elbow bumps and fist bumps instead.

In some cases, these gestures are cute and entertaining. But the performances can also be seen as inauthentic because our new communication forms are unfamiliar. Other, more natural reactions are becoming more pronounced as we show attention to others. We sometimes lean forward to demonstrate that we're interested in what someone is saying, but it isn't considered a primary way of connecting. We've pulled out second-string behaviors and use them because they are more natural to us. They're spontaneous and authentic, which is what non-verbal communication is supposed to be. Non-verbal communication is almost as necessary as the words we speak. Our tone of voice, eye contact, facial expressions, and body language are cues to how we feel. According to the Klein College of Media and Communication, these signals are crucial to how humans communicate because they help us navigate our relationships with others. Non-verbal communication is so rooted in how we understand the other person that if we have a difference between what we're saying and how we're behaving non-verbally, we almost always trust the nonverbal. Non-verbal communication also encompasses space and touch: how close you get to someone or allow them to get to you.

The pandemic disrupted all of this. We'll likely never go back to "normal," so it is important to remember that what is "normal" changes over time, even without pandemics. The pandemic created new etiquette, too. For example, long-standing social graces have always dictated that if you accepted the RSVP saying you would attend an event, you must do so. However, in our new normal, you can change your RSVP to decline at the last minute if you test positive for COVID, and most people will understand. We started to make some changes in our homes, too. Many of us now use air kisses to greet our guests, and some encourage guests to remove their shoes upon entering our homes, and we invite them to wash their hands before eating. And there's really no reason to go back to touching our glasses during a toast or blowing out birthday candles on a cake served to guests. Some of these things are already norms in many other cultures, but they are becoming more commonplace in our country.

The pandemic accelerated people's non-verbal communication and heightened their attention to media and technology. Research into how cell phones and the like affect how we communicate shows that we are so oriented toward our devices that we find it harder to want to engage with other people in person. It's a concern. When we predominantly use devices to communicate, we aren't exposed to those non-verbal cues that stimulate empathic responses. Because of the pandemic, we were pushed into an online existence. While we are getting better at reading the people we live with, we are getting a lot worse at connecting and reading people we interact with via technology. Young people are internalizing these norms and will probably stay with them in a way that older people like myself will flow in and out of. Given the shift to instant communication, we're actively discouraged from being face-to-face with others. The situation has severely affected society and the way we relate to one another. Connecting through snippets might be okay for saying things like, "I'm thinking about you" or "I love you," but they don't work for learning about each other or really connecting and understanding one another. The meaningful conversations we have with others help us learn about ourselves too. Not taking the time to have in-person conversation compromises our abilities to be self-aware and introspective. For kids, those skills are the foundation of development.

Some of the things we do now with our devices are things that we would have found odd or unsettling a few years ago, but they've quickly become the norm. It's just how we do things now. For example, no one I know calls to order takeout. Many of us do our grocery and other shopping online, too. We use our app and place our orders. In the comment section, we request the deliverer ring the bell and leave our goods on the front porch, so we don't have to interrupt the flow of our household when a real person arrives.

We're a crazy bunch. We are connected to the outside world twenty-four hours a day, seven days a week, three hundred and sixty-five days a year, but we rarely talk to new people and are getting good at ignoring the people we know, too. People are so distracted by real life that they text and email during corporate board meetings. They text, shop, and go on Facebook, Twitter, and Instagram during classes, presentations, and meetings. Parents text and email during meals while their children complain about not getting Mom's and/or Dad's full attention, yet these same kids deny each other their full attention. Some people are so ingrained in their habits that they don't recognize how they are pulling apart critical social graces. All this is doing is creating a new way for us to be alone together. We say we want to be with each other and connect, but we also want to go to more exciting places at the same time. We want to go in and out of places because we are driven by the fear of missing out — FOMO. Some people think that's a good thing, but we are hiding from each other. Across the generations, people can't get enough of each other if and only if they can have each other at a distance, in amounts they can control. Cultural Analyst Sherry Turkle calls it the Goldilocks effect: not too close, not too far, just right. But what might feel just right for that middle-aged executive can be a problem for an adolescent who needs to develop face-to-face relationships. Turkle goes on to say that conversations take place in real time, and you can't control what you're going to say, so texting, emailing, and posting allow us to present ourselves as we want to be. We edit, delete, and retouch our face, voice, flesh, and body. Turkle reminds us that human relationships are rich, messy, and demanding. And when we clean them up with technology, one of two things can happen: we sacrifice conversation for mere connection, or we short-change ourselves, and over time, we seem to stop caring.

Nowadays, most people I know would rather text than talk. This prevents us from having rich conversations. After a while, we become accustomed to superficial exchanges, and eventually, we end up distancing ourselves from some of our friendships altogether. Some pundits think texting and online conversations are appealing because so many of us are lonely and, at the same time, afraid of intimacy. Our online and texting relationships help us feel connected in ways we can control, and they give us companion-ship without the demands of friendship. One of the critical ingredients of feeling cared for is knowing that you have been heard. Listening is crucial to a successful relationship. That's why social media is so appealing. Hundreds, thousands, maybe even millions of people "listen" to what we have to say. This is why we are addicted to our devices. Sadly, we now expect more from technology and less from each other.

Our new techno world has some positives, too, so don't give up faith. Many of us are getting better at using our devices, which may benefit society in the long run. Technology can lead us to do better and learn more about our lives, communities, politics, and the planet. An old proverb says, "necessity is the mother of all invention." It implies that when we have no other choice than to complete a task or survive a crisis, we will find a way to do so. All of humanity's discoveries and creations were discovered due to man's need and desire to make the world a better place.

Ingenuity was at the forefront when the pandemic was testing us in every way possible. We were forced to stop all of our daily routines.

When the shock of the pandemic crisis abated slightly, we recognized that we could resume some of our activities through technology. Business leaders from hundreds of industries across the globe had to re-evaluate and re-invent their business models. Zoom, Teams, FaceTime, and other applications became vital players in helping industries generate commerce and keep people employed. This trend has continued and has significantly improved the quality of life for millions of people around the world. Remote working arrangements have allowed parents to spend more time with their families. The hybrid model gives employees the flexibility and freedom to choose the days they're coming into the office and the days they're working from home. More flexibility leads to a balanced workload, participation in team activities, and higher work-life satisfaction. In addition, engaged employees produce better outcomes, which increases profitability. Plus, involved and happy employees tend to stick around longer. Hybrid and remote work models reduce costs to employers, too. Companies need fewer desks, computers, printers, and other office supplies. They save money on utility costs as well. All this adds to the profitability of each company. Employees can save more money, too – from wardrobe costs to commuting costs to coffees, lunches, and dinners. Many industries have benefitted from the rise of hybrid and remote access. For example, fitness centers and exercise groups started meeting online and have continued the trend. Evidence shows that digital fitness is bringing more people into the world of workouts, helping them overcome some of the main hurdles that have stopped them from signing up in the past. Now, the inactive, the self-conscious, and the time-poor are signing up for digital fitness in droves, growing the market and creating opportunities for everyone in the exercise club space.

The pandemic also challenged local governments on many levels, including a pivot to holding remote meetings for health and safety reasons. Some local governments have transitioned back to in-person public meetings but found there was more public engagement by offering a hybrid option. Combining remote and in-person attendance in public meetings has many benefits for communities and the public. Online meeting platforms allow people to access and participate in discussions from their homes or workplaces. Providing both virtual and in-person meeting options appears to improve equitable access to local government. Individuals who cannot attend a public meeting in person due to a disability, work, small children in the house, or other commitments can choose the virtual option. At the same time, anyone who does not have the technological capability to participate online can opt for in-person attendance. All of this helps us stay connected to the issues that matter most. It allows us to contribute to our communities and gives our lives purpose.

The changes we've experienced in communication since the pandemic are remarkable. We have access to more information, and accessing meaningful experiences is almost effortless. All of this is rewarding, but there is nothing worthier than being with people in person. We cannot deny the primal need for connection. Intimate person-to-person conversations are more critical than ever. If you can't be together in the same place, then stay in touch with people by phone. Hearing people's voices makes us feel more connected, understood, and loved. The written word also offers a meaningful bonding experience, but it can't be accomplished in cryptic forms like texting and emojis. If we truly want to express our hearts' desires, we need to put pen to paper. It seems archaic, but remember how loved you felt after receiving such things.

Returning to normal after the pandemic has been a slow process. It is important to remember that what is "normal" changes over time, even without pandemics. Technology is making a bid to redefine human connection —how we care for each other and how we care for ourselves, and it's giving us opportunities to affirm our values. I'm optimistic. Social and digital media are sure to remain important for the foreseeable future. But they will never replace face-to-face interaction. Communication matters and should not be trivialized, whether in-person or through technology. We've examined in great length the nuances required for effective in-person dialog so let's look at ways to communicate effectively through modern-day means.

Texting is here, and it's here to stay—most people under the age of 55 report that texting is their most preferred communication method. Yet texting cannot convey the elements of speech required to understand emotions, like the tone of voice, gestures, facial expressions, and body language. A well-intentioned, rushed reply or poor punctuation can lead to misconstrued messages and feelings. Whether you're texting a friend, colleague, or customer, following texting etiquette can go a long way toward avoiding hurt feelings, embarrassing situations, and misunderstandings. What follows are some guidelines to abide by.

First, think of texting as a conversation. If you would respond in a person-to-person exchange, then react accordingly in the text. Acknowledge that the message was received and send a simple "thx" to signal the end of the conversation. Keep your messages brief. If you have a lot to say, make a phone call. Respond to a text by texting back or with a phone call. Don't text anything confidential, private, or potentially embarrassing. And don't be upset if your text doesn't get an immediate response—you can't know when the recipient will read the message. If you don't hear something within a few hours, call and speak person to person. It will go a long way in building a good relationship with them.

Most importantly, never text to inform someone of sad news or to end a relationship. Be a grown-up. Show kindness, be courteous, and deliver the information in person or by phone.

Social Media

In our world of sound bites, texting, and tweeting, we must demonstrate our morals and intelligence as best we can. If we surf the net, we interact daily with people with different experiences, cultures, perspectives, and power levels. It's important to remember that when we connect with people on social media networks, we are joining a community. As in any society, you must treat people respectfully and kindly and acknowledge their boundaries. There are countless online platforms, and navigating the onslaught can be overwhelming. The people running these shows encourage us to share, tag, and connect widely, instantly, and daily. We can get caught up in that pressure and lose track of how our postings affect others. Keep in mind that everything you do online is public and permanent. If you don't want Mom, Dad, Gramma, or Papa to see it, don't post it.

You also want to remember when to post something. Your employer doesn't want to see a TikTok video of you dancing while you are at work. There are basic principles of social media ethics and etiquette. Before you post something online, ask yourself a few questions. Are you venting or ranting? Complaining can feel good, but it doesn't help anything, and no matter how justified you feel, it never presents you in a positive light. Don't make yourself look foolish by gossiping or saying negative things about other people. Also, don't jump to conclusions if you aren't sure about something. Not everything should be displayed on social media. Consider the feelings of the other person. Show gratitude and respect to others, and don't take anyone for granted. Respond and thank those who engage with you but remember, some notes should be given in person, by phone, or by email. Manners columnist Catherine Newman created a list of social media guidelines to follow. I liked them so much I am using them unedited.

Facebook

Don't post about yourself 24/7. It's the nature of the medium, of course. And, sure, we all want affirmation. But try not to make every update about you and you alone. Try not to troll too frequently for compliments or sympathy. Actually, try not to post too frequently, period.

Post only flattering pictures of other people. Just because you're cool with being posted wolfing an entire deep-dish pizza doesn't mean your cousin, who was right there with you, will share your sentiments.

Friend wisely. Don't extend a request to your supervisor or a client. "You don't want them ga-ga-gooing at your baby niece or commenting on your Oktoberfest pics," says Newman. And if they friend you? Adjust your settings as needed to keep at least a thin boundary between work and regular life.

Spare us your synced games. No offense, but we don't even want to know that you're playing Candy Crush Saga, let alone receive tedious, spam-like invitations to join you.

Abstain from vague Facebooking. If you want to share something, please do it. But skip the ambiguous cries for attention: "It finally happened;" "ER visits suck;" or that frowny little emoji.

Twitter

Mind your meh. The avocado toast you ate for breakfast? How much you hate Mondays? Unless you're a comic genius, a Nobel prize-winning neuroscientist, or Kate Middleton, your every mundane thought is probably not worth posting.

Apply the billboard test. Assume that everyone in the world can and will see everything you post (the drunken rant, the gross joke), says Newman.

Be responsive. This is the quid pro quo rule: If someone you know follows you, follow him back; if someone tweets something nice about you, favorite it.

Don't request retweets. Make the most of your 140-character limit and followers will want to share your tweets all on their own, without your asking.

Instagram

Edit your photos. You went to Arizona and saw dozens of saguaro cacti that were uncannily human-shaped! Unless you're a professional cactus photographer, nobody wants to see more than two photos (or one).

Give credit where it's due. Don't post other people's photos or quotes without clear attribution. This means no screen grabs, even if you have the best intentions. Instead, use a repost app to properly credit others for their own content.

Restrain your use of hashtags. A hashtag can provide a funny or interesting interpretation for your photo viewers. But more is not merrier, and overuse of them is a common pet peeve.

Think of the future you. Your tastes will change, as will your sense of humor, your idea of TMI, and your interest in privacy—but your photos will live on forever. Once more, with feeling: Use caution when posting.

Snap Chat

Remember that the pics are not necessarily fleeting. "People can take screenshots of your snaps before they disappear," says Newman. "And those screenshots will then *not* disappear. Enough said."

Be wary of potential embarrassment. That goes for other people—and yourself. Just because this point can never be stressed enough: A nude snap is not going to do you any favors.

Don't take screenshots of other people's snaps. Creating permanent evidence violates the spirit of the medium. Folks using the app mean for their snaps to be transitory, and you should respect that intention.

Tik Tok

Don't post sensitive information. It may seem contradictory because TikTok is about putting yourself out there. Still, you should never reveal where you live or give detailed personal information about your habits, lifestyle, contact information, and so on. Keeping personal information private is the first rule to learn before using any social media. Remember that what is published no longer belongs to us. Every time we upload a video, make a comment or take any action on social networks, this content essentially becomes their property. Even when we delete them, they might not be taken completely off the platform.

Be careful what you publish. Taking into account the above, we should never, not even in private chat rooms, circulate content that could in any way embarrass us or third parties. In addition to possible legal consequences, we must remember that when we publish something online, we lose control of it. Individuals, companies, governments, etc., are constantly trying to get their hands on our private information, often for unsavory and life-changingly bad motives. We don't need to be paranoid, but we do need to be careful.

The most important thing we can do in life is to be respectful of real people – those who are right in front of us. Shut your gadgets off and interact with them in person because, unfortunately, all this socializing with technology can contribute to social isolation. Social isolation is another unintended and severe consequence of the lockdown. Social isolation is often used interchangeably with loneliness, but they are not the same. You can be lonely in a crowd, but you will not be socially isolated.

Loneliness is described as a state of solitude or being alone. It is a state of mind that causes people to feel empty, alone, and unwanted. Lonely people often crave human contact, but their disposition makes it difficult to connect with others. Researchers suggest loneliness is associated with poor social skills, introversion, and depression. According to experts, we don't have to be alone to be lonely. For example, a college student might feel lonely despite being surrounded by roommates and other peers. A soldier beginning their military career might feel lonely after being deployed to a foreign country, despite being constantly surrounded by other troop members. The death of someone significant in a person's life can also lead to feelings of loneliness. Loneliness can also be attributed to internal factors such as low self-esteem. People who lack confidence in themselves often believe that they are unworthy of the attention or regard of other people, which can lead to chronic loneliness and isolation.

Isolation is defined by the number of in-person interactions a person has, and loneliness is an individual experience. While the terms may have slightly different meanings, both can be painful experiences and harmful to the individual experiencing them. Social isolation – the absence of social interaction — can lead to loneliness. Many things, such as loss of mobility, unemployment, or health issues, can trigger the state of being cut off from society. Isolation can include staying home for lengthy periods, having no access to services or community involvement, and having little or no communication with friends, family, or acquaintances. Some people may be physically able to go out and meet people but are inhibited from doing so by factors such as depression, social adversity, grief, or becoming a caregiver for a loved one. These aspects can be barriers to forming and maintaining social networks, and any of them can lead to loneliness and isolation. The effects of social isolation on communication are that the less contact we have with others, the more we become suspicious of others. This can make people defensive. It can lead to a vicious spiral where isolation leads to suspicion, which begets defensiveness and reinforces the fear, leading to further isolation as a self-fulfilling prophecy. Social isolation is not something to take lightly. It has been shown to cause a number of severe mental health conditions. Among them are anxiety, depression, and post-traumatic stress disorder symptoms.

A twist here is that we can also go from connection to isolation by not cultivating a climate for solitude. We've been wired to believe that solitude is our enemy. The truth is solitude is necessary for our well-being and success. Solitude can be a very positive feeling that helps bring us into a state of balance. Our mental health and personal growth need to learn how to spend time alone. One of the most significant benefits of solitude is that it allows us to understand more about ourselves.

Research has come to prove that there are several long-term benefits to solitude. It allows people to find their voice. In a world where information is available at our fingertips, and everyone has an opinion to share, sometimes it's gratifying to trust that we alone have the answers we seek—all it takes is to build the habit of looking within ourselves. The more we learn to escape external influences, the more comfortable and confident we feel about who we are. This confidence, in turn, will project in the future decisions you will make.

Solitude can boost your creativity too. A recent study found that people who enjoy solitude tend to be more creative. Personally, I really appreciate my alone time. It allows me to rewind, reflect, and, more so, let my imagination wander. When I am alone, I often get my best ideas. I've heard many people say their best ideas come while in the shower, likely because it's the only "alone time" they give to themselves. It turns out solitude gives us opportunities to plan our lives too. We prepare for business meetings and upcoming vacations. We design and reflect for work and fun—but why don't we do the same for our dreams, aspirations, and personal lives? It's always a good idea to take a break from the rhythm of rush and reflect on whether we are living a life true to ourselves and our goals.

Finally, solitude can improve our mental well-being. Studies have shown that people who learn to find comfort in solitude tend to be happier, experience lower levels of stress, and are less likely to have depression. In short, it's the best form of self-care.

Moving Forward Together

So, where do we go from here? The solution to ending misunderstood texts, insensitive social media posts, social isolation, and loneliness is getting people back to in-person conversation. While social and digital media are sure to remain important for the foreseeable future, they will never replace the importance of real-time interactions or understanding the flow of conversation or body language. You've read a lot about how to accomplish meaningful connections with others, and now it's time to put what you've learned into action. Let's review how to improve your ability to communicate with others effectively.

Stay out of judgment. Do not judge or mentally criticize the speaker or what they are telling you. Doing so can compromise your ability to take in what is being said. You can evaluate what was stated after the speaker is finished talking, but don't do so while they are speaking. Let them finish their train of thought, and don't be a sentence-grabber. Interrupting the speaker or stopping them mid-sentence is disrespectful and can change their thought patterns and quickly destroy a productive conversation.

Be an active listener. Active listening shows the speaker that you're interested in and important to you. Active listening techniques help you to understand what was communicated correctly. Paraphrasing the speaker shows you heard and understood what they said. Non-verbal cues, such as nodding, eye contact, etc., are helpful to the speaker and allow them to dig deeper inside to tell you more. Again, don't interrupt the speaker. Let them finish their thought whether you agree with them or not. Be attentive and relaxed – don't get distracted by your thoughts and feelings. Don't rehearse what you will say after the speaker is done talking. Think about what the other person is saying rather than what your response will be. Effective listening is a skill that is frequently undervalued in our society. Good communication skills require both effective speaking and listening. By being an attentive listener, you can understand more and improve relationships.

Be concise. Convey your message in as few words as possible. Do not use filler words, and get straight to the point. Rambling will cause the listener to tune out or be unsure of what you are talking about. Avoid speaking excessively, and avoid using words that may confuse the audience. Don't repeat yourself. Utilizing the spotlight to express your idea in multiple ways is rude.

Use non-verbal cues. It is important to practice proper body language, use eye contact, utilize hand gestures, and watch the tone of voice when communicating with others. A relaxed body stance with a friendly style will aid in making you look approachable to others.

Be confident. What you say and your communication with others say a lot about how you see yourself. Being confident can be as easy as maintaining eye contact and having a relaxed body stance. Try not to make statements sound like questions, and avoid sounding aggressive or demeaning.

Be open-minded. In situations where you disagree with what someone says, whether with an employer, a co-worker, or a friend, it is important to sympathize with their point of view rather than simply try to get your message across. Respect the opinions of others and never resort to criticizing those who disagree with you.

Be respectful. Respecting and acknowledging the viewpoints of others is an essential aspect of effective communication. Respectfulness can be shown by simply paying attention to what they say, using the person's name, and not getting distracted by outside influences. The other person will feel appreciated and valued, leading to a more honest and productive conversation.

Succeeding in relationships, whether they're personal or professional, requires good communication skills. You need to know what you want and how you will attain it. Being an excellent communicator can help you achieve your goals and deepen connections with others. Respectfully and effectively articulating your wants and desires will give you a significant advantage in conversations and in life. Don't shy away from discussing problems respectfully or requesting more information to provide clarity. These are good human relations skills. They help in being understood and in helping understand the needs of those around you.

Final Thoughts

L istening is vitally important. Unfortunately, it is not a widely taught skill, and learning how to do it effectively can be physically and mentally taxing. In the aftermath of the pandemic, with the rise of online communication, it's never been more critical or challenging for people to be good listeners. This book was designed to offer tips to help you become a more active listener. My goal was to break down the skills involved in listening, and show how you can improve them. Becoming a great listener can be divided into two facets that come together seamlessly to allow the listener to be compassionate and effective.

The first aspect of listening is adopting and expressing an attitude of compassion. The second is developing specific listening skills and techniques to listen effectively. This book focuses on getting into a compassionate listener's mindset. Most of the time, we are so consumed in our thoughts that we do not take the time to step into the world of others to see things through their eyes.

To be great listeners, we need to be willing to humbly and momentarily put aside our perspectives and opinions, and hear from the person in front of us. The attitude of humility and genuine interest equips us to postpone our agenda and tune in to what the speaker is saying, with the intention of understanding. Listening is more than just hearing; it is a willingness to actively participate in another person's life by listening to them with compassion. The attitude of compassionate listening is embodied in this one rule: don't try to problem solve.

During an Oprah Winfrey interview, the Buddhist monk Thích Nhất Hạnh said, "Deep listening is the kind of listening that can help relieve the suffering of another person. You can call it compassionate listening. You listen with only one purpose: to help him or her to empty his heart. Even if he says things that are full of wrong perceptions, full of bitterness, you are still capable of continuing to listen with compassion. Because you know that listening like that, you give that person a chance to suffer less. If you want to help him to correct his perception, you wait for another time. For now, you don't interrupt. You don't argue. If you do, he loses his chance. You just listen with compassion and help him to suffer less. One hour like that can bring transformation and healing. Deep listening helps us to recognize the existence of wrong perceptions in the other person and wrong perceptions in us. Wrong perceptions should be removed by deep listening, compassionate listening, and loving space."

When someone tells us about a difficult situation, it can bring out our desire to problem-solve. But most of the time, people just want relief by talking through their pain. When we allow people to get their feelings out, they will experience healing. Understandably, our first instinct is to try to fix the issue, but most of the time, offering a solution can be damaging. More than a solution, the person experiencing a dilemma or difficulty needs the presence of another person willing to simply be with them.

The strategies found in *If You Love Me, You'll Listen to Me* are designed to help you love others in a way that can help them feel seen and heard. Instead of problem-solving or advice-giving, try to tune in to what the person is experiencing. Seek to really understand what they are going through and what emotions they are feeling. Exhibiting the willingness to sit with someone during their struggles sends a message of unconditional acceptance to that person. When we listen and seek to truly understand, we say, "I accept you as you are, even when you are stressed, depressed, or anxious, and I value you no matter how you feel." Human emotions are not problems, and they cannot be solved. Emotions are processed through expression, and when you ask about those emotions, you create an opportunity for processing and validation. Although it might feel right to jump into problem-solving or advice-giving, it is a sure way to invalidate the speaker and crush your connection. We are social and emotional beings that thrive on human connection. If someone wants your advice, they will likely ask for it. Advice-giving in and of itself is not bad, but listening and reflecting your understanding to the speaker first is essential, and problem-solving can come later, like, way later. Implementing this golden rule of listening becomes much easier when we have a humble attitude complimented by the practical skills and techniques discussed in this book.

Listening to our body, mind, and spirit gives us a better opportunity to be fully available to others. The study of self is a lifelong pursuit. Understanding ourselves and our behaviors is critical to a fulfilling existence. As poet Maya Angelou said, "When we know better, we do better." Your attitude is a tremendous tool that can set you up for success or put you on the fast track to failure. Let go of your insecurities.

Holding on to the belief that you "aren't good enough" will not allow you the capacity to give others what they need most in times of difficulty and dilemma. Always embrace an attitude of humility and generosity; remember, all of us want to be sincerely seen and known. At the same time, we are terrified of what might happen if we allow ourselves to be seen and known. There is nothing more extraordinary you can give someone than the gift of *your* human presence, of *your* heart full of compassion, of being someone willing to sit in solidarity with the discomfort of the ones you care about and love. This is truly the gift of listening. It is not simply being silent and allowing your ears to hear. It is participating in the life of another through actively showing them, "you matter to me, your experience matters to me, your emotions matter to me, and I am willing to listen." Communicating in this way invites them to be themselves in an authentic way. It has often been said that the greatest gift one can give a friend is their life, and there are countless stories of people who have given their lives so their loved ones could survive. To build on this belief of sacrifice, we should consider that one's life can only be lived in the present moment. When you give another human your full and undivided attention, even for a moment, you give them your life, for life can only be lived in the now. By letting go of your insecurities and humbly believing in the power of your presence, you allow yourself to become a source of healing through solidarity. This is the essence of compassion, "to suffer with." By embracing your own human value, you allow yourself to give another the gift that all of us long for, to be known, seen, and accepted. This type of presence and belief in the power of the human spirit opens up the opportunity to extend profound empathy.

Imagine what kind of family you can create and how you can strengthen other relationships by slowing down to hear what people tell you. The beautiful connections you design with your inner circle will have a ripple effect, making you responsible for a better society. But please, don't stop with reading this book. Continue investing in yourself because the surest way to achieve a better quality of life and be successful, productive, and satisfied is to prioritize investing in your personal growth. Investing in your knowledge and skills can take many forms. Extra classes, advanced degrees, and relevant certifications are all valuable investments. But so are workshops, conferences, and webinars; many are free, so take advantage of them as often as possible. Read books, and watch TED talks and YouTube videos. There is a fountain of creativity within you that has likely never been tapped or certainly hasn't been used to its highest potential. So please, never forget to nurture your mind and body to have more energy, knowledge, compassion, ideas, strength, and physical and mental endurance. You can spend your money on fleeting things or invest in yourself with eternal rewards. Give yourself experiences you will remember forever. Doing so will provide you with the strength to empower others, the eyes to see opportunity, and unconditional love to do good for yourself and others.

Thank you for reading my book. I hope it initiates something inside you that prompts you to listen to yourself and the people you love compassionately. Being an author was never something I dreamed of. When I began this undertaking, I thought it would be fun – and easy.

Well, I can assure you it was nothing of the sort. There were countless internal battles to overcome, and many days were spent in self-doubt. It took me far, far, far longer than it should have to complete my musings about why and how to have meaningful conversations. During the process, I recognized that I, too, have a lot to practice when making quality connections with others. I also realized that I'm not much of a writer either. Who knew? Sure, I could have abandoned this book project altogether, but I like to finish things I start. So here we are at the end of this labor of love. I'm not particularly pleased or displeased with how it came together, but I am proud – and happy that I finished it.

I'm also grateful for all the experiences I relived while writing this. I was reminded of many fond and not-so-fond memories. I was brought back to experiences and people who changed my life for the better. I feel ever so fortunate. But I also know as I've wandered through this life that I've made mistakes and unintentionally hurt people I care about and love. There's nothing to be done now except accept it, ask forgiveness from those I've hurt and offer forgiveness to those who may have hurt me. It helps to recognize that we're all human and can get past anything by showing grace to one another.

To forgive
Is not to forget
To forgive
Is really to remember
That nobody is perfect
That each of us stumbles

When we want so much to stay upright
That each of us says things
We wish we had never said
That we can all forget that love
Is more important than being right

To forgive is really to remember
That we are so much more
Than our mistakes
That we are often more kind and caring
That accepting another's flaws
Can help us accept our own

To forgive is to remember
That the odds are pretty good that
We might soon need to be forgiven ourselves
That life sometimes gives us more
Than we can handle gracefully

To forgive Is to remember
That we have room in our hearts to
Begin again, and again, and again

Acknowledgments

Thank you to all the people who believe in me. Jeff, you're at the top of the list. You sacrificed a great deal for this project. I am grateful beyond words. I will love you forever. I am thankful for the marriage retreat we attended that sparked the idea for this book. It opened my mind and helped me see the value of creating safe conversations to get the love we want – and need. Finally, I want to acknowledge my children, siblings, cousins, and friends who see my shortcomings and love me anyway. I love you more.

About the Author

Jeanne Hope Johnson lives in New Jersey with her husband, Jeff, and their dog, Duke.

Reading List

- *Free Range Kids* by Lenore Skenazy

- *Take Back the House* by Dr. Karen Latimer

- *SPARK* by Dr. John Rately

- *Getting the Love You Want – A Guide for Couples* by Dr. Helen LaKelly Hunt and Dr. Harville Hendricks

- *Parenting Inc.* by Pamela Paul

- *Parenting Without Fear* by Paul Donahue

- *Tell Me More* by Kelly Corrigan

- *The 7 Habits of Highly Effective People* by Stephen Covey

- *The Four Agreements* by Don Miguel Ruiz

- *The Gifts of Imperfection* by Brené Brown

Made in the USA
Monee, IL
12 February 2025